At Issue

How Should the U.S. Proceed in Afghanistan?

Other Books in the At Issue Series:

Adaptation and Climate Change
Affirmative Action
Animal Experimentation
Are Teen Curfews Effective?
Can Busy Teens Suceed Academically?
Child Pornography
Club Drugs
Do Abstinence Programs Work?
Do Infectious Diseases Pose a Threat?
Do Tax Breaks Benefit the Economy?
Ethanol
Fast Food
Is Racism a Serious Problem?
Is Selling Body Parts Ethical?
Nuclear Weapons

At Issue

How Should the U.S. Proceed in Afghanistan?

Stefan Kiesbye, Book Editor

GREENHAVEN PRESS
A part of Gale, Cengage Learning

Detroit • New York • San Francisco • New Haven, Conn • Waterville, Maine • London

Christine Nasso, *Publisher*
Elizabeth Des Chenes, *Managing Editor*

© 2009 Greenhaven Press, a part of Gale, Cengage Learning.

Gale and Greenhaven Press are registered trademarks used herein under license.

For more information, contact:
Greenhaven Press
27500 Drake Rd.
Farmington Hills, MI 48331-3535
Or you can visit our Internet site at gale.cengage.com

ALL RIGHTS RESERVED.
No part of this work covered by the copyright herein may be reproduced, transmitted, stored, or used in any form or by any means graphic, electronic, or mechanical, including but not limited to photocopying, recording, scanning, digitizing, taping, Web distribution, information networks, or information storage and retrieval systems, except as permitted under Section 107 or 108 of the 1976 United States Copyright Act, without the prior written permission of the publisher.

For product information and technology assistance, contact us at

Gale Customer Support, 1-800-877-4253
For permission to use material from this text or product, submit all requests online at www.cengage.com/permissions

Further permissions questions can be emailed to permissionrequest@cengage.com

Articles in Greenhaven Press anthologies are often edited for length to meet page requirements. In addition, original titles of these works are changed to clearly present the main thesis and to explicitly indicate the author's opinion. Every effort is made to ensure that Greenhaven Press accurately reflects the original intent of the authors. Every effort has been made to trace the owners of copyrighted material.

Cover image © Images.com/Corbis.

LIBRARY OF CONGRESS CATALOGING-IN-PUBLICATION DATA

How should the U.S. proceed in Afghanistan? / Stefan Kiesbye, book editor.
    p. cm. -- (At issue)
    Includes bibliographical references and index.
    ISBN 978-0-7377-4424-8 (hardcover)
    ISBN 978-0-7377-4425-5 (pbk.)
    1. United States--Foreign relations--Afghanistan--Juvenile literature. 2. Afghanistan--Foreign relations--United States--Juvenile literature. 3. Afghan War, 2001---Juvenile literature. 4. Nation-building--Afghanistan--Juvenile literature. 5. United States--Foreign relations--Pakistan--Juvenile literature. 6. Pakistan--Foreign relations--United States--Juvenile literature. I. Kiesbye, Stefan. II. Title: How should the United States proceed in Afghanistan?
    E183.8.A3H69 2009
    327.730581--dc22
                                                                    2009009745

Printed in the USA
    2 3 4 5 6   30 29 28 27 26

Contents

Introduction	7
1. Slowness in Providing Early Aid Has Allowed a Taliban Resurgence *Paul M. Rodriguez*	10
2. U.S. Withdrawal Would Leave Afghanistan in a Shambles *Alex Thurston*	17
3. A Failed U.S. Strategy Helps the Taliban Win Local Support *Paul Rogers*	23
4. United States Needs Patience and Pakistan's Help to Overcome the Taliban *Lisa Curtis and James Phillips*	29
5. The United States Must Work at the Local Level to Encourage Democracy *Jesse Aizenstat*	43
6. The Afghan Army and Parliament Must Provide National Unity *Beth Cole and Kiya Bajpai*	48
7. NATO Must Commit to Afghanistan's Future *Bruce Riedel and Karl F. Inderfurth*	55
8. NATO Must Help Afghanistan and Its Neighbors Cooperate *Joschka Fischer*	59
9. The Course of U.S. Action Must Run Through Pakistan *Fred Kaplan*	63

10. The United States Must Not Destabilize Pakistan *Jim Lobe*	68
11. Covert Operations Cannot Substitute for Sound Policy *Patrick Cockburn*	73
Organizations to Contact	78
Bibliography	81
Index	87

Introduction

In January 2006, the United States launched a missile attack on a mountain village in Pakistan. The targets were Osama bin Laden's deputy, Ayman al-Zawahiri, and other al-Qaeda members. "The missiles were deadly accurate," the *Guardian*, a British newspaper, reported afterwards, describing the scene: "Three ruined houses, mud-brick rubble scattered across the steeply terraced fields, the bodies of livestock lying where thrown by the airblast, a row of newly dug graves in the village cemetery and torn green and red embroidered blankets flapping in the chilly wind." Yet the militants the U.S. forces were targeting were not in the destroyed houses. Instead eighteen villagers died, among them four children.

Pakistan, considered an ally by the George W. Bush administration, distanced itself from the operation and "announced it would file a formal protest with the Americans." In the aftermath of the incident, "thousands of local men marched in a series of protests . . . , one crowd attacking the office of a US-funded aid group," the *Guardian* reported.

A week earlier the U.S. military, searching for al-Qaeda hideouts, had killed eight people in the North Waziristan region of Afghanistan. When the *Guardian* interviewed villagers, Shah Zaman, a jeweler who lost three children in the attack, said, "This is a big lie. . . . Only our family members died in the attack. . . . They dropped bombs from planes and we were in no position to stop them . . . or to tell them we are innocent. I don't know [al-Zawahiri]. He was not at my home. No foreigner was at my home when the planes came and dropped bombs."

Since then, the United States has stepped up its attack on Pakistani villages suspected of harboring al-Qaeda members. But since U.S. troops are not allowed to cross the border from Afghanistan into Pakistan, American forces have relied increasingly on unmanned drones to carry out the air strikes. While technologically advanced and largely accurate, drones are highly controversial weapons. They can strike in remote and inaccessible regions, but miscommunication can endanger U.S. soldiers on the ground, and drones carry the risk that faulty intelligence can lead to the death of innocent people.

In September 2008, shortly after a territorial violation by U.S. helicopter commandos carrying out an attack, missiles fired by several drones killed sixteen people, including four women and children, according to London's daily *Independent*. "Fifteen to 20 wounded people, most of them women and children, had been taken to hospital in Miranshah, the main town of North Waziristan, doctors said." The United States claimed to have killed several Taliban and al-Qaeda fighters, while people on the ground contended that "no foreign militant was killed."

Expressing her concern about the use of drones, Elizabeth Rubin, in an article for the *New York Times*, wrote,

> While these [drones] are saviors to the soldiers, they cannot distinguish between insurgents and civilians. I went to Afghanistan last fall with a question: Why, with all our technology, were we killing so many civilians in air strikes? ... According to Human Rights Watch, NATO [North Atlantic Treaty Organization] was causing alarmingly high numbers of civilian deaths—350 by the coalition, compared with 438 by the insurgents. The sheer tonnage of metal raining down on Afghanistan was mind-boggling: a million pounds between January and September of 2007, compared with half a million in all of 2006. After a few days, the first question sparked more: Was there a deeper problem in the counterinsurgency campaign? More than 100 American soldiers were killed [in 2006], the highest rate since the invasion. Why were so many more American troops being killed?

These examples show the dilemma of U.S. forces trying to fight an enemy that so far has proved either elusive—as in the case of al-Qaeda—or has gained strength and influence—as is the case with the Taliban. Critics contend that U.S. troops are fighting in regions they have little knowledge of, and don't have clear targets—every missile strike might kill a few fighters, yet it also undermines the American efforts to win local support for their missions. While fighting the enemy, they argue, soldiers are also creating resistance among the population, ill will, and outrage.

The Western world favorably greeted the removal of the Taliban following the 2001 invasion, and—in contrast to the war in Iraq—there has been little doubt about the justification of the initial air strikes. The Taliban, after their fight against a Russian invasion had ended in 1988, erected what many say was a cruel and oppressive regime. Furthermore, they gave shelter to al-Qaeda terrorists and harbored their leader, Osama bin Laden, who engineered the 9/11 attacks. Today, though, concerns are growing over the U.S. strategy. Many in the international community fear that Afganistan, once seen as a success, might fall prey to the renewed efforts of a Taliban-led insurgency. The drone attacks are an important piece in the puzzle that is the war on terror. With continued attacks on insurgents—which so often kill civilian bystanders—critics maintain that the United States might not only be losing credibility and international support, but the moral high ground as well—not to mention the war itself.

Slowness in Providing Early Aid Has Allowed a Taliban Resurgence

Paul M. Rodriguez

Paul M. Rodriguez is the managing editor of Insight on the News *magazine.*

A big obstacle on the path to a functioning democracy in Afghanistan has been the failure of Western aid to deliver on many promises. Billions of dollars in aid has gone to the country, yet much of it is eaten up by overhead costs. Also, many aid groups do not communicate well with the other groups, leading to more wasted funds. The real losers in this situation are the Afghan people, many of whom do not have access to necessities, like water, security, or education.

Afghanistan: 34 degrees 36 minutes north latitude, 28.38; 68 degrees 55 minutes east longitude, 41.12. High in the mountains above the Crystal Lake of Qargha, where only a few months ago the reservoirs below were bone dry, people flock by foot and car and truck on Fridays to enjoy a unique type of picnic. It is for them as much a celebration of their freedom as it is a family outing of the kind one might find anywhere in the world....

This gathering ... provides an opportunity to spend time with hundreds of Afghans from all walks of life and to discuss

---

Paul M. Rodriguez, "Rebuilding Afghanistan," *Insight on the News*, July 8, 2003. Copyright © 2003 News World Communications, Inc. All rights reserved. Reproduced with permission of Insight.

the future of their country and the lessons that should have been learned among Westerners about the perils of nation building....

Afghans are appreciative of the hundreds of millions of dollars in international relief that has been poured into their war-ravaged country, not to mention the cost of sending in and maintaining the U.S.-led coalition of military personnel who provide what security there is and much-needed relief and reconstruction assistance.

During the course of nearly three weeks in the country, it is evident that people here at all levels of society are grateful to the United States. But as one of only a handful of Westerners ever to venture so far up into these mountains to spend time with Afghans and then visit with them in their homes, mosques, hospitals and bazaars, one does not miss the hazards as innocent questions are put directly.

"Who will protect our people" once the Americans leave, asks an old man as he watches beggar children traversing the dangerous towpaths along the rushing waters above Qargha. "Where is the aid that has been promised?" he asks....

Democracy is given lip service, but few understand the implications of this Western concept.

A Considerable Difference

Spending time separately with Westerners and Afghans made it clear that there was a considerable difference between what each group thinks needs to be done to rebuild an infrastructure that has been destroyed systematically. For instance, what should be done to build septic systems capable of preventing human waste from polluting the groundwater? The dangers are grave. Infant mortality is roughly one in four due to disease and malnutrition. Millions of land mines have been scattered over fields made barren by four years of drought and by the shocking decision of the Taliban to cut off water supplies to many agricultural areas as punishment to resisting tribes. Education was for years almost completely disrupted, resulting in 80 percent of women and somewhere between 60 and 70 percent of men being illiterate. . . .

A wide array of Westerners and Afghan officials tell Insight that somewhere up the line the decision has been made to keep the United States in the background while leaving the bulk of the aid work to the international bureaucrats, heavily laden with overhead that eats up 60, 70 and sometimes as much as 90 percent of funds targeted for aid on the ground. Afghans see this and express desperation. . . .

There are constant complaints about the U.S.-backed administration of President Hamid Karzai. He derisively is called the "Mayor of Kabul" and "Mr. Commission" because of his shrinking authority and penchant for announcing new studies as civil issue after civil issue reaches crisis, according to locals all the way up to his ministerial officers. . . .

Security is the key, say almost all of those interviewed. It makes no difference who provides that security and this raises troubling issues, because traditional warlords have men waiting eagerly at the outskirts of Kabul and other cities to provide security for the millions who continue to pour into the country. Democracy is given lip service, but few understand the implications of this Western concept. "It's a hard road ahead," confirms Jean-Jacques Blais, a Canadian national who leads his country's mission on matters of constitutional reforms for Afghanistan. The chief problem he sees, confirmed repeatedly by Afghans, is that despite the severe crisis in infrastructure and public health the international relief agencies have widely divergent agendas based upon inappropriate models or irrelevant experience.

"This is to be expected," says the head of a European delegation who has been in country for months. An NGO chief adds, "You have to understand that there is a bureaucracy in play, and it takes huge sums of money to feed it." Even so, he expresses disgust at the waste and inefficiency he says is a major failure by groups such as his....

Building a Nation

Minister of the Interior Ali Jalali says the job of nation building that his government faces can be accomplished if the international relief agencies will begin to cooperate more fully and coordinate their services. But Jalali and [Mohamed Arif] Noorzai [the minister for frontiers and tribal affairs] confirm a sense of resentment among a growing number of Afghans who see the swarms of Land Cruisers driven by the international bureaucrats as a symbol of indifference and colonial intentions. There are other hot-button sentiments that frequently surface in conversations with Afghans. "We're tired of hearing the promises," laments an older man named Abdullah, a successful entrepreneur when he has goods to sell. A retired doctor who has practiced through many years of war agrees: "They come and make studies and promise to return with services and needed supplies. But all we get are more studies and more promises."...

Such criticisms may be valid to some extent, many Westerners here tell Insight, but they ignore hundreds and hundreds of projects to build schools, clinics, roads, electricity stations and other infrastructure. The problem, it seems, is a failure to coordinate such good works through a bold national plan of action and provide the people with progress reports that tie together local projects and national reconstruction, says a senior communications official in the Afghan government....

Despite your editor's repeated requests for formal interviews with President Karzai and some senior Cabinet ministers, "emergency meetings" or administrative snafus consistently got in the way. But this afforded access to midlevel bureaucrats who freely spoke their minds and provided access not only to government records but to filings by a variety of the internationals. These confirmed how confusing and difficult it has been to coordinate infrastructure programs and find workable solutions for many of the country's ills.

Karzai told Insight last year [2002] at a meeting at the Afghan Embassy in Washington that he was promised billions of dollars but that his country had seen very little of that directly. He also said it was hard even to find out what was being done. It's not that millions weren't pouring in, Karzai confided. "I'd just like to know where it all goes," he said.

Overall, $5 billion has been pledged in grants and loans for the reconstruction of Afghanistan since January 2002, with a reported $2 billion for 2002 alone. It seems like a lot of money, the Afghans say, but administrative overhead eats up some of the promised funds, and promised contributions are not always forthcoming or are tied to special programs such as police training or school construction.

This worries Noorzai. But, he says, "I believe a new nationalism has emerged and we are learning. But we must work together as a team. Afghanistan has been a war zone for most of the last 5,000 years, and this long-term fighting has led to survival based on tribal traditions that now must give way to a new national government. This can only come via security at the borders and a unity among the tribal peoples who must be part of the security force and have a role in government." . . .

> *Things have to change, and one of the key items is to allow Afghans to adopt Western models of government in ways that work within the culture.*

Application of Law Poses Many Obstacles

The deputy ministerial official, whose job is to help develop a system of laws for Afghanistan, just shakes his head. "The laws are screwed up and application of laws, such as they are, is uneven at best," he insists. "If it were up to me, I would do away with the import taxes for domestic use of machinery and goods to help foster growth. But the new law says there must be taxes on such imports even though there are no definable regulations to carry out the mandate." And warlords control the borders.

A businessman from Herat agrees and says he has been trying to free up about $250,000 in bakery equipment stuck at a customs warehouse in the western Afghan city. "I refuse to pay the bribes, the tricked-out fees, to free my goods," he defiantly tells Insight as he sits most of one day at the office of the finance minister in hope of getting a waiver. "I blame [Afghan President Hamid] Karzai for this, and he better get things fixed soon or the warlords will take over sooner than anyone thinks. . . . Such confusion in the central government only plays into their hands," Mohammed Sadqee says.

Muhammad Malam Mahmood agrees. It is his job, among many, to oversee the import duty fees and taxes. And he's frustrated, convinced as he is that these laws need to be expunged immediately to foster commerce in the country. . . .

Even so, Mahmood is a patriot and he puts it bluntly: "Things have to change, and one of the key items is to allow Afghans to adopt Western models of government in ways that work within the culture, not in ways that are required by the West or by people who don't know what they are doing or just because of politics."

"The Professor" Remains Moral Force for Unity

He is affectionately known as "The Professor." He is the leader of the Afghan National Liberation Front and briefly was the first interim president of the Islamic State of Afghanistan after the defeat of the Soviets. Sibghatullah Mojaddedi is a spiritual leader of a famous family in Afghanistan and they are patriots. . . .

Mojaddedi is a moral force for unity in a free Afghanistan. "This can only come about if we have strong leaders while we establish an education system that teaches the young the skills they will need to lead this country. We can make here a model for all Islamic nations that are wiling to be progressive and democratic," he says. "It is my profound wish to help make this happen." . . .

The Professor radiates hope. "We need the help of the international community and America to establish cohesive programs," he says. "We need their help now to restore medical care. Modern water and sewer systems are key infrastructure needs that must be addressed quickly. Plus adequate books and supplies to educate our children and update the skills of our people. This last will be the key. Education of the people and, especially, all of the children. They are our future now."

U.S. Withdrawal Would Leave Afghanistan in a Shambles

Alex Thurston

At the time of writing Alex Thurston was a graduate student in the Arab Studies Program at Georgetown University in Washington, D.C. From 2006 to 2007, he lived in Senegal as part of the Fulbright exchange program and studied Muslim youth movements in the capital city of Dakar.

In its efforts to resolve the problems it faces in Afghanistan, the United States has only three heavily flawed options. It could try to turn around the current decline and support development projects that would stabilize democracy, yet no coherent plan for such a commitment exists. It could maintain current troop levels and involvement, yet staying that course would only play into the hands of the Taliban. The final option is withdrawal with a multilateral diplomatic effort, but the danger a failing Afghan democracy might pose to the region, as well as to American interests, seems prohibitive.

In most of my writing I take strong stances, especially against unilateral military action. It is clear to me, for example, that the US should leave Iraq, albeit while launching a diplomatic initiative and taking other precautions to reduce potential bloodshed there. But the situation in South Asia is somehow more difficult for me to make up my mind on. Therefore I pose the question to you: Should the US withdraw from Afghanistan?

Alex Thurston, "Should the US Withdraw from Afghanistan?" *The Agonist*, 14 March 2008. Reproduced by permission of the author.

As I think through this, I'll lay out what I see as the three main options before us. But first, let me touch briefly on the broad pros and cons of withdrawal from Afghanistan.

The argument for withdrawal is largely predicated on the assumption that current military and development strategies in Afghanistan will not change enough, even under a Democratic administration, to realize the project of nation- and democracy-building that would be essential for any American "victory" in Afghanistan. The argument against withdrawal, on the other hand, assumes that the resurgence of the Taliban which would likely follow withdrawal would wound American prestige and threaten the integrity of NATO [North Atlantic Treaty Organization] at a time when both of these phenomena are perhaps important components of any potential stability in the world. Additionally, the argument against withdrawal also holds the US morally responsible for doing its best to fix the mess in Afghanistan before leaving.

[A "victory"] would require a sustained effort to bring conditions of justice, stability, and peace to Afghanis at the local level.

With this in mind, here are what I see as our three major options:

An Attempt at "Victory"

Remain in Afghanistan and attempt to "win" through nation-building and other development projects. I can imagine a scenario in which the United States and NATO, through a dramatic reversal of military strategy and overall approach in Afghanistan, could bring about stability and national unity in the country. This would involve, at the least, a rigorous effort to reduce civilian casualties to an absolute minimum, subsidies to pay farmers not to grow opium poppies, and development projects that employed large numbers of Afghanis at an attractive wage. It would also demand greater accountability from the [President Hamid] Karzai government as well as the US military and private US contractors operating in the country. Finally, it would require a sustained effort to bring conditions of justice, stability, and peace to Afghanis at the local level. In short, we would have to supplant the Taliban and undercut every aspect of its local appeal, from its ability to regulate local problems to its role in the drug trade. Underlying these strategies would be a more participatory and inclusive form of development work, such as that seen in microfinance networks, rather than the heavy-handed top-down approach that characterizes much of the US's development efforts. For example, putting Afghanis to work paving roads could represent an important step toward generating income for the people and creating infrastructure to lead the way toward further development. Above all, we would listen to Afghanis and implement their suggestions.

One counterargument to this strategy is that these ideas would meet with strong disapproval on the domestic front as politicians attacked "wasteful" expenditures in Afghanistan and accused the government of being soft on terrorists and drugs. This opposition could sway public opinion against the war completely, or provoke a return to earlier failed strategies.

Withdrawal from Afghanistan, if conducted properly, would be accompanied by major diplomatic initiatives on the part of [the] US and the EU.

Another counterargument is that no model for success exists, either in the military realm or the development sphere. When has the US successfully accomplished nation-building outside of Western Europe and Japan? critics ask. Is the situation in Bosnia, for example, comparable to the situation in Afghanistan? Furthermore, how could the ingrained and institutionalized habits of individuals and agencies in the US government, particularly the Departments of Defense and State, be altered so dramatically in a short period of time?

Continue with the Current Approach

If domestic support and institutional capacity for the development-heavy approach are lacking, but American leadership feels queasy at the thought of outright withdrawal, they could attempt to remain in Afghanistan without a major change in strategy. It is difficult to describe this option without sounding cynical, but the main argument in its favor is that if we are caught between the rock of withdrawal and the hard place of development strategies that lie out of reach, maintaining the status quo is a tempting course. Allowing the situation to limp along, or counting on an infusion of troops and resources when the US leaves Iraq, could minimize the Taliban's ability to maneuver and allow US prestige and NATO integrity to survive in the medium term.

The disadvantages here are almost too many to name. I believe that even with 100,000 more troops, it would be difficult to stabilize Afghanistan by force. Our current approach seems almost calibrated to turn Afghanis against us. Furthermore, without seriously addressing the destabilizing impact of our presence across the region, we risk provoking larger crises simply by remaining. This course's only real advantage is basically that it allows us, in the best case scenario, some time to think and see if a better option comes along.

A Complicated Withdrawal

Withdrawal from Afghanistan, if conducted properly, would be accompanied by major diplomatic initiatives on the part of [the] US and the EU [European Union]. After holding bilateral talks with Iran (something we would need to do for a variety of other reasons), we should invite Pakistan, India, Iran, and Afghanistan to a regional summit where we would offer each country specific incentives, inducing them to make contributions to building stability in Afghanistan. Involving other powers, such as Central Asian nations, China, and Russia, would likely also prove to be a good idea. Some manner of discussions with the Taliban would also need to take place, hopefully to find out if there is any way to reconcile their aims with those of the Karzai government and the international community. Finally, in an ideal situation the US would throw its weight behind a UN-led effort to create an institutional framework for stabilizing Afghanistan.

Additionally, the US would disengage from its current misadventures in Pakistan, as well as its allegiance to [Pakistani president Pervez] Musharraf, and lend its support to the democratically elected parliament. Through engagement with both Pakistan and India, the US would do its utmost to press for a solution to the Kashmir issue and establish greater regional cooperation.

Are we doomed to leave Afghanistan a failed state, just as we found it?

The major disadvantages here are that if the frameworks we set up failed—ie, if the Taliban overthrew the Karzai government by force and retook control of the country—both NATO's integrity and America's prestige *could* be severely damaged. While I have no sentimental attachment to NATO or American prestige as such, one could argue that in a dangerous and unpredictable world both NATO and America *could* represent important and positive forces. If the new century is to be characterized by a complex balance of powers among various rising giants, the EU, and the US, perhaps the postwar organs of Europe and America still have a role to play.

More importantly to my mind, the failure of "multilateral" operations in Afghanistan could discourage future attempts at multilateral military intervention in crisis situations. As someone who believes strongly that some genocides, such as the Darfur crisis, will eventually require military force to make them stop, I would be concerned at the prospect of a future where major powers become even more reluctant to stage interventions.

No Easy Solution

What I have spelled out here are three deeply flawed options. There are others, I imagine, and the ideas presented here are not mutually exclusive—the regional summit I propose in the withdrawal option, for example, could easily fit with the development-based strategy. Thinking through the problem of what to do about Afghanistan leaves me with a deep sense of pessimism. Again, while I believe that after a US withdrawal Iraq would eventually regain stability, I do not share that confidence regarding Afghanistan. Are we doomed to leave Afghanistan a failed state, just as we found it? And is that really a solution, given how other failed states—Somalia, Sudan, etc—are still destabilizing their neighbors and denying their inhabitants any chance of a meaningful or prosperous life?

Some of the best minds in America and the world have been thinking through the problems caused by our invasion of Iraq. I would encourage some of them to turn their sights on Afghanistan as well, which comparatively has received far less attention. Perhaps they'll come up with solutions more compelling than the ones I've offered here.

A Failed U.S. Strategy Helps the Taliban Win Local Support

Paul Rogers

Paul Rogers is a professor of Peace Studies at Bradford University in the UK and the author of Losing Control: Global Security in the Twenty-first Century.

Suicide killings and other attacks have risen sharply, but the American response of air strikes has caused many civilian deaths. At the same time, the Taliban have been able to establish themselves once again as an influential force. This has led to an increased activity of al-Qaeda operatives and threatens Afghan democracy. Pakistan, an official American ally, has done little to secure its borders with Afghanistan, and the Taliban are able to cross them and go into hiding, only to return with more fighters. Yet going to war in Pakistan seems out of the question, and an increase in the Taliban's influence seems likely.

On 7 July 2008 a suicide-bomber detonated a large car-bomb at the gates of the Indian embassy in Kabul, killing fifty-four people and injuring more than 140. The embassy stands in one of the most secure parts of Afghanistan's capital, yet this did not protect it from what security forces described as the worst bombing in the city since the termination of the Taliban regime in November 2001. Taliban sources denied that the movement was responsible, while Afghan sources implied (albeit without supporting evidence) a Pakistani intelligence connection. The high death-toll is in part at-

Rogers, Paul. "Afghanistan: State of Siege." *OpenDemocracy.net*, July 10, 2008. Reproduced by permission.

tributable to the fact that many people were queuing [lining up] at the embassy at the time; this may be a factor too in the Taliban reaction, for it has been a regular practice of the group to deny responsibility for attacks where large numbers of civilians are killed.

Whoever was responsible, the Indian embassy attack came at a time of escalating violence in Afghanistan marked by a number of high-profile paramilitary actions. These include an assassination attempt against President Hamid Karzai at a military parade on 27 April 2008, and the dramatic raid on Sarpoza prison in Kandahar which freed dozens of Taliban prisoners and which was followed by the seizure of several villages close to the city. A day after the embassy attack, a bomb was found on a bus carrying Indian workers in the province of Nimroz (where many Indian projects, including the strategic Zarang-Delaram highway project, are centred).

For the US forces, the biggest surprise has been the growth in Taliban activity in the eastern part of the country.

A Pattern of Killing

The seriousness of the situation in Afghanistan has led to the United States navy's redeployment of a carrier battle-group led by the aircraft-carrier USS *Abraham Lincoln* from the Persian Gulf to the Arabian Sea; this will enable US strike aircraft to provide further air-power in Afghanistan.

The problem with this response is the danger it carries of continuing the pattern of inflicting civilian deaths in misdirected air-strikes, which in turn provokes affected communities to turn against the coalition forces. The International Committee of the Red Cross (ICRC) estimates that in the period of 2–7 July 2008 alone, paramilitary violence and coalition military action together killed at least 250 civilians, and that deaths caused by US air power being a particular source of tension on the ground.

The question of deaths as a result of missile-strikes is a source of great controversy. In two recent incidents, for example, there is dispute over the identity of the dead Afghans. Local Afghan officials claimed that the fifteen people who died in a US missile attack in Kunar province on 4 July were civilians, while American spokespersons insisted that only militants were killed; Afghan officials were equally adamant that the at least twenty-seven victims of a missile-attack on 6 July included nineteen women and children, reportedly members of a group of around eighty or so people in a wedding party who were taking a rest while walking to the groom's house.

Whatever the true circumstances of these and other cases, the killing of civilians by coalition forces is deeply unsettling and has added to the anti-western mood in many parts of the country already hard-pressed by problems such as growing food insecurity. The pattern of civilian deaths also comes at a time when coalition sources are beginning to admit to the seriousness of the strategic predicament they face in Afghanistan.

Each year since the Taliban regime was ended, foreign troop numbers in the country have risen; the single greatest increase has been since early 2007, with 20,000 additional troops arriving to take the overall total to around 66,000. Despite this, the intensity of Taliban activity has also increased. Much of it is seasonal, with less fighting during the severe winter months, but even here there has been a change. In recent years, suicide-attacks in cities such as Kabul and Kandahar have increased overall, but they have also continued through the winter months.

For the US forces, the biggest surprise has been the growth in Taliban activity in the eastern part of the country. This region, close to the Pakistan border, has been garrisoned by US forces operating independently of NATO [North Atlantic Treaty Organization], and there have been frequent claims of progress [since 2006]. The US forces and spokespersons have made pointed references to the contrast between their "success" and the difficulties experienced by British troops in Helmand province and the Canadians in Kandahar.

Insurgents on the Rise

Now, though, the US claims are sounding less assured. The newly-appointed US military commander for eastern Afghanistan, Major-General Jeffrey J Schloesser, has highlighted the increased sophistication of the methods used by the insurgents as a factor in the rising violence. This has led to a near-doubling of the number of US troops killed in the country in the first six months of 2008 compared with the similar period in 2007. What has become particularly noticeable has been the more widespread use of roadside bombs, with tactics developed in Iraq being deployed in Afghanistan.

The escalation of violence in Afghanistan has two other elements. The first is a loss of support for the war in a number of NATO member-states that have committed troops. A Pew Global Attitudes Project survey conducted in a number of NATO countries in April 2008 (even before the violence intensified in the following two months) found majority support for the withdrawal of NATO forces—ranging from 54% to 72% in countries including France, Germany, Spain, Poland and Turkey.

The second element is the steady rise in power of Taliban and al-Qaida paramilitaries in western Pakistan. The Pakistan-based Taliban militias now have considerable influence in many of the border districts of Pakistan, including parts of the Federally Administered Tribal Agencies, and North Waziristan and South Waziristan.

This influence in turn has two effects. The first is that Taliban groups fighting in Afghanistan have safe havens across the border; but if US forces mount raids into western Pakistan this simply stirs up more anti-American feelings across the country.

> *American military and intelligence sources are reporting a marked increase in the involvement of foreign fighters with Taliban militias in western Pakistan.*

The second effect, and just as significant from a US perspective, is that the Taliban control has allowed al-Qaida to regenerate. An informed assessment is that there are as many as two thousand paramilitaries established in training camps in western Pakistan, up from several hundred [in 2005]. The issue has been complicated by differences of opinion within the United States over the need for US forces, whether CIA, special forces or regular military, to operate within Pakistan. This remains unresolved but has become even more complicated by the uncertainties of politics within Pakistan itself.

A "Winning Fight"

Pervez Musharraf remains president, though his diminishing influence means that his markedly pro-American outlook carries less weight. The coalition government remains in some disarray over the president and other issues, but its overall mood—reflecting an even stronger popular feeling—is unwillingness to allow greater US military involvement in the border districts. The bottom line, which is keenly recognised within the higher echelons of the Pakistani civil service, is that the population as a whole will simply not accept more US involvement. It has become a political non-starter.

The consequences for the US military are thoroughly negative. The senior NATO commander in Afghanistan, General David McKiernan, states, "The porous border has allowed insurgent militant groups a greater freedom of movement across that border, as well as a greater freedom to resupply, to allow leadership to sustain stronger sanctuaries and to provide fighters across that border."

American military and intelligence sources are reporting a marked increase in the involvement of foreign fighters with Taliban militias in western Pakistan. These include young men from Chechnya, Uzbekistan and the Gulf states; since March 2008 the numbers have increased (according to an unnamed Pentagon official) "from a trickle to a steady stream." This is part of a trend in which Pakistan and Afghanistan are now the focus of attention for paramilitaries intent on fighting western forces....

A Decisive Year

The accumulating result of these trends is a deteriorating security situation across much of southern and eastern Afghanistan, made worse by the Taliban/al-Qaida revival across the border. A forceful United States government might have insisted on taking the war to Pakistan, even against the overwhelming opinion against this within that country. But the George W. Bush administration is nearing the end of its term and is, in any case, far more preoccupied with Iran.

In April 2008 a number of analysts were suggesting that 2008 would be a decisive year for the seven-year war: either the Taliban would succumb to the overwhelming weaponry available to NATO and US forces, or the movement would increase its power. At the midpoint of the year, the latter view looks more accurate—so much so that Afghanistan might even exceed Iraq as an issue at the heart of the American presidential campaign.

United States Needs Patience and Pakistan's Help to Overcome the Taliban

Lisa Curtis and James Phillips

Lisa Curtis is a senior research fellow at the Heritage Foundation, focusing on analyzing America's economic, security, and political relationships with India, Pakistan, Afghanistan, Sri Lanka, Bangladesh, and Nepal. James Phillips is a senior research fellow for Middle Eastern affairs at the foundation's Douglas and Sarah Allison Center for Foreign Policy Studies.

While the United States is taking steps to increase troops and financial aid for Afghanistan, it will take a comprehensive long-term strategy to keep Afghanistan democratic and prevent the Taliban from once again establishing their regime. Government services, as well as police and army protection have to improve to convince the population that democracy is a viable option to Islamic rule. Attention should be paid to Pakistan, whose porous borders make militant groups' entry into Afghanistan, as well as their retreat, possible. Only a coordinated long-term effort, using diplomacy and military strikes, might provide the stability Afghanistan needs to counter the insurgents' attacks and become a peaceful democracy.

Afghanistan is a crucial front in the global struggle against the al-Qaeda terrorist network and Islamic radicalism. The United States-led coalition was unable to transform an

Lisa Curtis and James Phillips, "Revitalizing U.S. Efforts in Afghanistan," *Backgrounder*, October 15, 2007. Reproduced by permission.

overwhelming military victory in 2001 into a stable postwar political situation because of Afghanistan's fractious politics and shattered economic, state, and civil society infrastructures; a minimalist American approach to committing military forces and foreign aid; Pakistan's failure to crack down decisively on Taliban forces that have taken refuge in Pashtun tribal areas along the Pakistan-Afghanistan border; the Afghan government's failure to expand its authority and deliver services to rural Afghans; and a shortfall of economic aid, due in part to many countries' failure to fulfill their foreign aid pledges to Afghanistan.

The [George W.] Bush Administration made Afghanistan stabilization efforts a priority from when the Afghanistan Transitional Administration was formed in December 2001 until Hamid Karzai was elected president in October 2004. Since then, U.S. leadership on Afghanistan has waned, leading to decentralization and fragmentation of the international reconstruction and stabilization process. In addition, poor governance and corruption in the Karzai government have fueled popular discontent, which the Taliban has exploited.

The U.S. has pledged to increase assistance to Afghanistan significantly [in 2008 and 2009] (about $2 billion for reconstruction and $8.6 billion for security assistance), and in January [2008] extended the deployment of 3,200 U.S. troops in Afghanistan. These are steps in the right direction. But to ensure that Afghanistan does not again become a safe haven for terrorism, Americans must wage a long-term integrated political, military, and economic development campaign to convince Afghans that their interests are better served by an inclusive democratic government than by a radical Islamic regime.

Struggling to Extend Central Authority

Historically, Afghans have resisted strong centralized rule, whether by kings, communists, or the Taliban. Afghanistan is a complex mosaic of ethnic and tribal groups that zealously guard their independence. Afghanistan's difficult mountainous terrain has posed a formidable physical barrier to movement, communication, and the extension of central authority. Local leaders in each valley and plateau have long exhibited a prickly independence, suspicion of outside authority, and latent xenophobia.

All of these factors have made it difficult for Hamid Karzai, Afghanistan's first post-Taliban leader, to extend his government's authority much beyond Kabul and the northern areas that were hostile to the Taliban, primarily composed of southern Pashtuns. Although the charismatic Karzai remains a popular leader, there has been growing criticism of his government's failure to do more for Afghans outside the main cities and grumbling from the south over the perceived inadequacy of Pashtun representation in his government.

The size of the Taliban's fighting force remains unknown. Most of its fighters are part-time, mobilized ad hoc to fight against specific targets.

Pashtuns have historically played a leading role in Afghan politics. Karzai, a Pashtun leader from the powerful Popalzai tribal clan, has tried to stay above tribal politics and function as a truly national leader, but he has been handicapped by lack of effective political parties, the weaknesses of the embryonic Afghan government, and the continued strength of traditional tribal leaders, warlords, and local militias.

Despite these challenges, Afghanistan has made substantial political progress in a relatively short time. Under the Bonn Process, a constitution was drafted in 2003 that established a framework for building a democratic government. In October 2004, Hamid Karzai became Afghanistan's first elected president. A bicameral legislature consisting of the Wolesi Jirga (House of the People) and Meshrano Jirga (House of Elders) was elected in 2005. . . .

The Forgotten War

Although the United States dealt the Taliban a devastating military defeat in 2001, the radical Islamic movement has made a limited but significant comeback in recent years and threatens to endanger Afghanistan's hard-won progress. Bolstered by support networks anchored in the Pashtun tribal areas of Pakistan, the Taliban and allied insurgent groups have seeped over the porous border and gained control of a steadily increasing swath of Afghan territory. According to declassified intelligence, insurgent groups expanded the territory where they operate by more than 400 percent between 2005 and 2006. The number of insurgent attacks has steadily increased, rising from 1,558 in 2005 to 4,542 in 2006. Although attacks have occurred throughout the country, most are concentrated in the Pashtun heartland in southern and eastern Afghanistan.

The size of the Taliban's fighting force remains unknown. Most of its fighters are part-time, mobilized ad hoc to fight against specific targets. According to one estimate, the Taliban deployed 2,000 to 4,000 full-time fighters in 2005. Taliban strength has undoubtedly grown since then. The Taliban remains incapable of holding ground against U.S. or NATO [North Atlantic Treaty Organization] forces but is successfully waging a campaign of guerrilla warfare by harassing government and coalition military forces, intimidating Afghan and foreign civilians, and attacking government officials and facilities.

The Taliban's strategy and tactics have evolved gradually since it regrouped and launched the insurgency in the spring of 2002. It initially attacked coalition forces with relatively large bands of up to 100 fighters in 2002 and 2003, but bloody setbacks inflicted by superior Western firepower and devastating air strikes dissuaded it from continuing such tactics. The growing U.S. military presence, which rose from less than 10,000 troops in 2003 to nearly 20,000 in 2004, also may have led the Taliban to change tactics by deploying smaller bands of less than 10 fighters, which can maneuver and launch small-scale hit-and-run attacks while evading detection and counterstrikes.

The Taliban and other insurgent groups have increasingly moved away from directly challenging coalition forces to using roadside bombs and suicide bomb attacks similar to those conducted by Iraqi insurgents. Roadside bombings increased from 783 in 2005 to 1,677 in 2006, while suicide bombings surged from 27 in 2005 to 139 in 2006. [In 2007], there have been 123 suicide bombings as of the end of August. Such attacks have not been as effective in Afghanistan as they have in Iraq, and more than 90 suicide bombers in the past two years have failed to kill anybody but themselves, perhaps because they were not trained as well as the predominantly Arab radicals who have conducted most of the bombings in Iraq.

Additional Influences in Afghanistan

Iran has played an increasingly troublesome role in Afghanistan, as it has in Iraq. Tehran has a long history of supporting Afghan client groups against the central government in Kabul.... Tehran has continued to supply these groups, some of which have joined the Karzai government, with money and arms as a hedge against American influence.

Iran has also sought to expand its proxy network in Afghanistan to include elements of the Taliban movement, its longtime enemy. [In 2007], coalition forces in Afghanistan have intercepted Iranian arms shipments to the Taliban on April 11, May 3, and September 6. U.S. Undersecretary of State R. Nicholas Burns announced in June [2007] that the U.S. had "irrefutable evidence" that Iranian Revolutionary Guards armed the Taliban. The intercepted arms have included "artillery shells, land mines ... rocket-propelled grenade launchers," and "sophisticated Chinese-made HN-5 antiaircraft missiles," which led Washington to complain to Beijing. Although Iran has a history of ideological hostility toward the Taliban, it has a strong geopolitical interest in aiding its war against the United States, their common enemy.

A Hydra-Headed Insurgency

In addition to the Taliban, the insurgency is waged by ... other major Afghan groups and by foreign Islamic radicals. ...

In addition to these Afghan groups, several hundred Muslim militants from other countries have joined the insurgency inside Afghanistan. Most of them are from neighboring Pakistan, Uzbekistan, and Tajikistan, but smaller numbers come from Egypt, Saudi Arabia, Sudan, Yemen, Iraq, Somalia, and Chechnya. The foreign militants are reportedly better trained, better equipped, and more professional fighters than the Afghans, who often fight only on a part-time basis.

All of these groups operate from sanctuaries in Pakistan. The Taliban leader Mullah Omar is reportedly based near Quetta in Pakistan's Baluchistan Province. The Taliban, Hezbi Islami, the Haqqani network, and many foreign Islamic militant groups including al-Qaeda also have support infrastructure in Pakistan's Federally Administered Tribal Areas (FATA), particularly in North and South Waziristan. The Taliban and other radical Islamic movements are more popular in Pakistan than in Afghanistan, and they conduct most of their financing and recruiting activities on the Pakistani side of the border. The Pakistani government, which has limited authority in the tribal agencies of the FATA, has often turned a blind eye to the activities of Afghan insurgent groups based in its territory.

Prioritizing Pakistan–Afghanistan Relations

The West's ability to defeat al-Qaeda capabilities and ideology rests on a strategy that integrates diplomatic and security efforts toward Afghanistan and Pakistan and focuses more intently on improving relations between these two key countries. The Afghanistan Freedom and Security Support Act of 2007 . . . acknowledges this linkage and authorizes the President to appoint a special envoy to promote closer Afghanistan-Pakistan cooperation.

Washington will need to take a more proactive role in mediating disputes between Afghanistan and Pakistan, prodding both countries to develop a fresh strategic perception of the region based on economic integration, political reconciliation, and respect for territorial boundaries. To achieve stability in the region, Pakistan must root out Taliban ideology from its own society and close down the madrassahs (religious schools) and training camps that perpetuate the Taliban insurgency.

For its part, Afghanistan must acknowledge the sanctity of the border dividing Pashtun populations between the two countries and ensure adequate representation of Pashtuns in the Afghan government. Pashtuns in Afghanistan number about 12 million, making up 42 percent of the population, while about 25 million Pashtuns live in Pakistan, making up around 15 percent of the population.

It is imperative that the U.S. work with Pakistan to develop a more effective strategy to neutralize the terrorists operating in this region.

British colonialists purposely divided the ethnic Pashtun tribes in 1893 with the Durand Line, which is now the 1,600-mile porous Afghanistan-Pakistan border. Afghanistan at one time claimed Pashtun tribal areas in Pakistan and has never officially recognized the Durand Line. Pakistan in the past has countered Pashtun nationalism within its own borders by promoting pan-Islamic extremism in Afghanistan.

Peace Meeting Is First Step

The Afghanistan-Pakistan peace jirga held in Kabul in early August [2007] was a first step in bringing local leaders from both sides of the border together in face-to-face talks. While no one expected immediate breakthroughs, the gathering was an important step in building confidence between the hostile neighbors. About 700 Pakistani and Afghan delegates focused on terrorism as a joint threat to the two nations and urged their governments to make the war on terrorism an integral part of their national policies and security strategies.

One highlight of the jirga was President [of Pakistan] Pervez Musharraf's admission during the closing ceremonies that Afghan militants received support from within Pakistan. His statements represented a welcome departure from past rhetorical barbs blaming Afghanistan's woes entirely on President Karzai. Musharraf's remarks demonstrate that the two sides have made some limited progress in improving relations since the historic tripartite meeting hosted by President George W. Bush in September 2006, where the Afghan and Pakistani leaders could barely stand to look at one another.

Islamabad's assistance in the capture and killing of several senior Taliban leaders may have contributed to the decreased hostility between Presidents Musharraf and Karzai. Mullah Akhtar Osmani, formerly the head of Taliban operations in southern Afghanistan, was killed in December 2006 by an air strike; Mullah Dadullah was killed by the British in May [2007] in Helmand Province; Taliban Defense Minister Mullah Obaidullah was arrested in Pakistan earlier [in 2007]; and key Pakistani Taliban leader Abdullah Masood was killed by the Pakistanis in Baluchistan Province. . . .

Developing a Joint Strategy

Despite Pakistan's counterinsurgency efforts in the FATA over the past four years, the region is still one of the world's most dangerous terrorist safe havens. Given the connections among recently exposed international terrorist plots, the instability in Afghanistan, and the terrorist training camps in these tribal agencies, it is imperative that the U.S. work with Pakistan to develop a more effective strategy to neutralize the terrorists operating in this region.

Beginning in late 2003, the Pakistan military deployed 80,000 security forces to the tribal areas to disrupt the terrorists, but these military operations also damaged traditional tribal institutions, increased radicalism in the region, resulted in the deaths of several hundred Pakistani soldiers, and stirred up opposition in the broader Pakistani population. Fighting between Pakistani government forces and insurgents in the border areas intensified in the spring of 2006, resulting in numerous Pakistani civilian casualties. The terrorists also resorted to brutal and systematic assassinations of local tribal leaders who cooperated with government forces.

On September 5, 2006, because of the growing problems with military operations in the FATA, President Musharraf announced a "peace deal" with tribal leaders of the North Waziristan Agency that included an end to offensive Pakistani military operations in exchange for the tribal rulers' cooperation in restricting Taliban and al-Qaeda activities. The Pakistan government sought to restore the traditional form of governance in the region and to co-opt tribal elders and political representatives through an infusion of economic assistance for new roads, hospitals, and schools.

Al-Qaeda Is Strong in Pakistan

Recent statements by senior U.S. intelligence officials reveal that the Pakistani peace deals in the FATA have not achieved the desired objectives and in fact have allowed the region to develop into an al-Qaeda stronghold. Cross-border attacks against targets in Afghanistan's nearby Khost and Paktika provinces rose from 40 attacks in the two months before the agreement to 140 attacks in the two months afterward. U.S.

intelligence officials noted in mid-July [2007] that al-Qaeda remains as strong as ever due to its safe haven in Pakistan's tribal borderlands. Pakistani extremists also took advantage of the decreased military pressure by attempting to impose strict Islamic edicts in the region—the same tactics employed by the Taliban in Afghanistan in the mid-1990s. The extremists have sought to close down girls schools, barber shops, and video stores by force and are increasingly challenging the writ of the government, even in some of the settled areas of the Northwest Frontier Province.

The revelations by U.S. officials of al-Qaeda's resurgence in the tribal areas coincided with the storming of the Red Mosque in Islamabad, which left at least 100 dead. Reports indicate that there were links between the leadership of the Red Mosque and al-Qaeda elements in the tribal areas. The combination of events led Pakistan to send fresh military reinforcements to the region, to reactivate military checkpoints, and to conduct limited military operations.

While Pakistan's willingness to go back on the military offensive in the tribal areas is welcome, Islamabad's efforts alone are unlikely to address the serious threat from the region, U.S. and Afghan forces have repeatedly pursued insurgents to the border but are banned from crossing into Pakistan. Coalition forces have alerted Pakistani authorities to the movement of retreating insurgents across the border but in the past have elicited little Pakistani counteraction. However, since August [2007] Pakistani forces have actively engaged militants in the FATA, killing hundreds of terrorists while suffering significant military casualties.

Washington needs to convince Islamabad to work more closely in joint operations that bring U.S. resources and military strength to bear on the situation and employ a combination of targeted military operations and economic assistance to drive a wedge between Pashtun tribal communities and international terrorists. A large-scale U.S. troop invasion of

Pakistan's tribal areas would be disastrous for the Pakistani state and would not provide a lasting solution to the problem. A more effective strategy involves working cooperatively with Pakistan's military to assert state authority over the areas and, once they are secure, provide substantial assistance to build up the economy and social infrastructure. The [Bush] Administration is already moving in this direction with a pledge of $750 million over five years to develop the tribal areas. The security and development challenges in Pakistan's tribal areas are similar to what the coalition forces face in Afghanistan; that is, the need for state institutions to establish the upper hand before international development assistance can begin to flow to the region.

Over the longer term, U.S. assistance should encourage political reform that incorporates the institutions of the tribal lands fully into the Pakistani system. Some have argued that the Pakistan military is loath to implement political reform in these areas and that only the democratic parties would move in this direction. In late July [2007], Pakistan People's Party leader Benazir Bhutto filed a petition with the Pakistan Supreme Court seeking enforcement of the Political Parties Act in the FATA, which would extend Pakistan election laws to the region and encourage political activity. Political parties are currently prohibited from functioning in the FATA, although 12 seats in the National Assembly (the lower house of parliament) and eight seats in the Senate are reserved for FATA members. The petition claims that since the political parties are not allowed to field candidates for elections, the mosques and madrassahs have been able to assert undue political influence in the region.

At the same time, the U.S. and Pakistan need to take aggressive military action when they receive intelligence on high-value targets. The U.S. has already directed two aerial strikes—in January 2006 and October 2006—in the Bajaur Agency of the tribal areas reportedly aimed at al-Qaeda number two, Ayman al-Zawahiri. Although those particular strikes were widely condemned in Pakistan for the civilian casualties involved, decisive precision strikes will sometimes be necessary....

Waging a Long-Term Campaign

The Taliban poses more of a long-term political and ideological threat than a short-term military threat. OEF [Operation Enduring Freedom] and ISAF [International Security Assistance Force] forces have won important battlefield victories over the Taliban and have killed or captured many of its leaders, but the Taliban cannot be defeated merely by military means. The Afghan people are the center of gravity in the struggle against the Taliban and its militant allies. Ultimately, only the Afghans, not Westerners, can decisively defeat the Taliban. The U.S. and its allies need to convince Afghans that their long-term interests are better served by an inclusive democratic government with substantial economic aid from the West than by a radical Islamic regime. Building the capacity, effectiveness, and public support of the Afghan government should be the highest priority.

> *Consolidating a stable Afghanistan that is free from Taliban influence and ideology will be expensive and will require a patient, long-term, integrated political, military, and economic strategy.*

The counterinsurgency campaign in Afghanistan cannot be won without establishing a government that responds to the needs of Afghans in threatened areas and earns their trust. To help to fill the gap until Afghan government services can be extended to more areas, the U.S. and its allies should increase the number of Provincial Reconstruction Teams (PRTs) beyond the current 25 and provide them with more funding to bring immediate and visible improvements to the lives of

Afghan civilians, especially in areas threatened by a resurgent Taliban. Afghan officials should be deployed in PRTs in greater numbers to put an Afghan face on the operations and improve liaison with local, provincial, and national bureaucracies.

The Taliban came to power in 1996 in large part because of widespread frustration with the anarchy and lawlessness that followed the 1992 collapse of the communist regime. Today, many Afghans in the provinces are frustrated with the perceived lack of tangible benefits provided by the Kabul government.

The Afghan National Police are severely underfunded, poorly trained, and poorly equipped. Many go months without pay because of corruption and problems with the payroll system. This encourages them to extort bribes and makes them vulnerable to corruption. Germany, the lead nation for building the police force, has mistakenly tried to build a conventional state police force rather than a mix of paramilitary police and local forces. The United States should take over lead responsibility for reforming the police, purge corrupt leaders, and deploy more police trainers and embedded advisers to improve the effectiveness and reliability of the police. Given the extensive criminal activity in many areas, the police should be expanded beyond the current target of 82,000 officers.

The Afghan National Army (ANA), which has a current strength of about 36,000 troops, should also be expanded beyond the Bonn Conference target of 70,000 troops, which was set before the Taliban resurgence. Afghan Defense Minister Abdul Rahim Wardak has called for expanding the ANA to 150,000 men, which seems a more realistic number, especially in preparation for when ISAF forces start to draw down.

Pay for army and police recruits should also be raised to attract better candidates, increase retention rates, and reduce temptations for corruption. Afghan soldiers are currently paid about $70 per month—less than what Taliban fighters are paid and far less than the estimated $4,000 per day cost of maintaining a NATO soldier in the field in Afghanistan....

Consolidating a stable Afghanistan that is free from Taliban influence and ideology will be expensive and will require a patient, long-term, integrated political, military, and economic strategy. However, the alternative of allowing Afghanistan to revert to its pre-9/11 status of control by the al-Qaeda-friendly Taliban is not an option. To reach U.S. goals in Afghanistan, the U.S. will also need to prevail over Pakistani resistance to ending the Taliban's role in Afghanistan. This will require deft diplomacy that recognizes the need for improved Pakistan-Afghanistan relations through increased trade and economic linkages and joint political endeavors.

The United States Must Work at the Local Level to Encourage Democracy

Jesse Aizenstat

Jesse Aizenstat was a fourth-year political science student at the University of San Diego at the time of this writing.

It is impossible for the United States to provide the help and support needed to protect civilians, uphold democracy, and successfully fight the Taliban. Instead, it is up to Afghanistan to take over security. American forces should help increase Afghan troop levels, as the army has proved—unlike the police—to be reliable. Also, the United States should give aid to help strengthen the infrastructure and create jobs.

Even if you were hiding in a cave in Afghanistan, I still think you could hear the roar from the [2008] American presidential election. Without rest, [Senators] Barack Obama and John McCain passionately disagree on virtually every policy issue we face, but the war in Afghanistan is different: "Time for a troop surge," or "Refocusing on the Central Front"—they both want more troops. In a year, all these election promises will be over, and the next author for America's newfound saga in Afghanistan will begin. But just because these candidates' "grand plans" sound good on the campaign trail, doesn't mean that they will be the "right plans" for the future. Afghanistan is a vastly complex place that cannot be understood from the American political stump.

Jesse Aizenstat, "US Must Reconsider Goal, Position in Afghanistan," *Daily Bruin*, September 21, 2008. Reproduced by permission.

I don't want to sound pessimistic about America's hopes for Afghanistan, but we must appreciate that we have limits as foreign occupiers. It is up to the Afghans to ultimately purge government corruption and settle on a system that works for them. In the meantime, the West can provide some security and aid, but we do not have the legitimacy or the know-how to tackle these problems for them. This is why the U.S. needs to take a fresh look at Afghanistan for what it is, not for what we think we can make it.

Setting the Stage

From a Western perspective, it seems absurd that we haven't routed the Taliban. How could this medieval band of Pashtun fighters, armed with little more than a Kalashnikov and a Koran, withstand our Western force? Well, to start, our forces are having a hard time understanding how to handle these rural Afghan societies where the Taliban seek refuge.

The Taliban is trying to . . . bleed our forces by luring us to fight on the village level.

As Canadian [brigadier-general] Denis Thomson said in an interview [in September 2008], "I don't know that the Taliban [is] getting stronger. . . . The difference is they're not holding any of the ground they're attacking us on." So despite our air force, tanks and modern weaponry, it appears that we are about to enter a new phase of the insurgency. Realistically, how deep into tribal Afghanistan are we going to chase these guerillas? Or more to the point, what repercussions might we face by doing so?

In 1979, [Soviet leader] Leonid Brezhnev and the Politburo [Soviet ruling body] moved the Red Army into Afghanistan. Major cities like Herat and the capital, Kabul, were conquered. Looking back, it seems obvious why the Soviets, at the peak of the technologically-hyped Cold War would overlook rural Afghan tribal society. However, this same tribal society birthed the mujahideen, or "freedom fighters," who by using guerrilla tactics were able to bleed the Soviets into exiting Afghanistan. This is what the Taliban is trying to do today: bleed our forces by luring us to fight on the village level—a level that by definition, we foreigners do not understand.

It wasn't always supposed to be such a cumbersome military production in Afghanistan. During the 2001 American-led invasion, we were able to oust the Taliban with a light cocktail of American Special Forces and a band of anti-Taliban warlords known as the Northern Alliance. This coalition proved both efficient and effective in booting the Taliban from their role as the "legitimate" government in Kabul.

So what happened? Today's critics will say that this "light footprint" era has failed in Afghanistan. They argue that increasing our current troop level of 31,000 as of September [2008], is necessary to defeat the so-called, "Taliban revival." But an Iraq-type "surge" as these critics often insist on, will not bring peace to Afghanistan. Rather, it runs the risk of inspiring Afghan nationalists to sympathize with the Taliban, thus making it near impossible for us to run operations in the villages that the Taliban now hides in.

The American-led air strikes on Aug. 22 [2008] that killed 90 civilians were possibly the result of a Taliban loyalist deliberately feeding our intelligence false information. Our troops are not trained for this non-conventional resistance campaign. Sending more troops will not make things better in Afghanistan and will continue to weaken our political hand in the region.

Redefining Our Military Policy

Frankly, the American public and our allies are uncertain about broadening our mission in Afghanistan, especially after the Caucasus flare-up between Russia and Georgia [in 2008].

The Taliban know this, and they will continue to wage an insurgency to try to make it "not worth it" for the coalition. Germany and the Netherlands are already looking to significantly reduce their military commitment and, it's not impossible to understand why. Instead of trying to fight a costly counter-insurgency campaign, we would do better to focus on counter-terrorism. Besides, no one learned how to fly a plane into the World Trade Center from tribal Afghanistan anyway.

In a perfect world, we would like the central government of Afghanistan to secure its borders and assert its legal legitimacy in both urban and rural areas. But until then, some academics have suggested that a "troop redistribution" is needed to help transition the whole country under Kabul's control. While this proposal sounds nice, it would stretch our resources in a way we cannot afford. This would be a typical mistake by the West.

Instead, we should look to the experts—the Afghans. One initiative would be to give the Afghan army a greater role in day-to-day security. Backed by our Special Forces, this combination would work to bolster the legitimacy of Kabul and help to discredit brewing colonial conspiracy theories.

Recently Defense [Secretary] Robert Gates came around to this very notion. Gates endorsed a plan that would provide $20 billion to double the size of the Afghan Army to 120,000 active-duty troops. Unlike the notoriously corrupt Afghan police, the Afghan Army with its high morale, is willing and battle-tested. Of course, they will be dependent on American trainers and equipment, but this is an investment worth making. Afghans are proud people and with the right support, they will show that they are competent to defend themselves against the brutality of the Taliban.

Looking to the Future

A strong military can help provide security for Afghanistan. But it will be the rebuilding that will determine what, if any, legacy we might leave behind. We must remind ourselves that we do not have the will, or the desire to occupy this country forever so we should focus on empowering Afghans to carry out local-level building projects that would directly improve their lives.

The more we try to "take over the situation" the less incentive we create for the Afghan government to take charge and reform.

Large-scale projects may be easier for us, but as [former occupiers] the British and the Soviets might say, that is just not how Afghanistan works. We should look to simple projects that include all of Afghanistan's ethnic fronts to create jobs and continue to avoid ethnic tensions.

As for Kabul, Western funding and know-how has been able to set up an effective central bank with a stable currency. Some might scoff at the concept of democracy in Afghanistan, but they do have an elected parliament, which has been perhaps the most effective method yet for distributing government aid to the countryside.

We can help rebuild Afghanistan, but we must recognize our limits. Both presidential candidates should realize that the more we try to "take over the situation" the less incentive we create for the Afghan government to take charge and reform. We should not continue to tarnish our credibility and weaken our global authority by trying to do something that we simply cannot do.

The Afghan Army and Parliament Must Provide National Unity

Beth Cole and Kiya Bajpai

Beth Cole is a senior program officer and Kiya Bajpai is a research assistant at the Center for Post-conflict Peace and Stability Operations at the United States Institute of Peace. Cole also coauthored The Beginner's Guide to Nation-Building.

The United States invaded Afghanistan without a clear plan for reconstruction, thus slowing down the postwar development of the country. Aid for civilians was slow and insufficient, and political progress was undermined by a fragile infrastructure and a lack of control in the tribal areas. To act before the window of opportunity closes, development aid must increase. Also, the Afghan government needs to establish itself in pro-Taliban regions. Together with a strengthened army, the government needs to strive for national unity.

The international community and the [Hamid] Karzai government [of Afghanistan] are losing "a battle of confidence" among the Afghan people. Three new trends signal that the momentum is changing: the precipitous increase in Iraqi-like suicide bombings, the unprecedented rise in hostility among ordinary Afghans toward Westerners, and the expanding number of Afghans who are "on the fence" on the question of whether to support the government or the Taliban.

Beth Cole and Kiya Bajpai, "Afghanistan Five Years Later: What Can the United States Do to Help?" *United States Institute of Peace.* November 2006. Reproduced by permission.

With the window of opportunity to change direction rapidly shrinking, the United States needs to take dramatic steps to spur the delivery of governance, security, and development in order to stabilize Afghanistan. Only by injecting the country with much needed resources and building local Afghan capacity can the United States help the government in Kabul establish its legitimacy and win back support from the Afghan people.

> *The Afghanistan Compact ... is a "great road map" for a stable and economically viable state but will remain a paper plan without a dramatic increase in resources.*

This was the general consensus from the first of two sessions in a four part series at the U.S. Institute of Peace to examine U.S. efforts in Afghanistan five years after the fall of the Taliban. The October 19, 2006, meeting of the Afghanistan Working Group featured Deborah Alexander, former special adviser to the U.S. embassy in Kabul; Jonathan Landay, a McClatchy Newspapers journalist with extensive reporting experience in Afghanistan; and Mercy Corps' George Devendorf, just back from visits with local staff in Afghanistan. On October 25, 2006, Alex Thier, senior Rule of Law adviser in the Institute's Center of Innovation for Rule of Law, was joined by *Washington Post* deputy foreign editor Pamela Constable. These discussions were moderated by Beth Ellen Cole, Coordinator of the Afghanistan Working Group at the U.S. Institute of Peace.

A Lack of Resources

When the United States went into Afghanistan in 2001, the focus was on military operations and not reconstruction. "We went into Afghanistan with a plan to track down terrorists and kill al-Qaeda," observed Deborah Alexander, who was among the first Americans at the U.S. embassy in Kabul after the fall of the Taliban. "That's not a reconstruction or stabilization plan." Finally, in 2004, an Integrated reconstruction plan put forth by the U.S. Department of State and the U.S. Agency for International Development (USAID) laid out a vision for Afghanistan. Despite this vision, U.S. economic, political, law enforcement and diplomatic efforts remain "stovepiped" and require more coordination. For example, the $130 million investment in elections was an important first step, but the $8–$10 million currently allocated by the United States for democracy and governance in Afghanistan—a nation of 30 million people—is woefully inadequate. The U.S. embassy has also been severely understaffed, making it nearly impossible to integrate reconstruction and civil military efforts. While its ranks have grown from 25 to nearly 400 in the past few years, this cannot compare with the size of the staff in the Baghdad embassy. The Afghanistan Compact, agreed to by donors in January 2006, is a "great road map" for a stable and economically viable state but will remain a paper plan without a dramatic increase in resources.

A rise in civilian casualties from Western military operations and insurgent tactics coupled with the anemic pace of development has caused deep resentment of the West and the Karzai government. Devendorf reported that this new hostility makes it more difficult for anyone associated with the government or the international community to operate, as insurgents are increasingly targeting Afghan nationals who work for international NGOs [nongovernmental organizations], NATO [North Atlantic Treaty Organization] and U.S. operations within the country. Landay predicted that these insurgents, who retreated in past winters, will have enough ammunition and manpower to remain in urban areas and thus escalate attacks through the winter and spring. As Constable noted at the second session, "This is a new Taliban."

Moreover, the Afghan national police program requires an immediate infusion of resources to attract new recruits, pay salaries, provide proper equipment, and deploy experienced mentors to facilitate the development of effective police forces with accountable leadership. Some areas have absolutely no recruits. A majority of the existing force has succumbed to corruption and nepotism. Security still remains largely dependent upon U.S. and NATO forces, which recently assumed command of the International Security Assistance Force (ISAF), and a nascent but improving Afghan National Army. There are only 8,000 ISAF troops in the volatile south, an area of nearly 77,000 square miles.

Drugs and Corruption

According to Constable, Afghans say their worst problem is corruption. Instead of police protection and justice, the people are faced with extortion and abuse on a daily basis. The lack of trust in the government has left a void that is now being filled by the Taliban. Decisive action against corrupt officials is needed to change a situation where impunity reigns. Though the drug trade was virtually eliminated in 2000 by Taliban forces, it has begun "creeping, then soaring back" under local warlords, said Constable. A solitary focus on eradication will only harm the local farmers who are trying to feed their families. Calls have been made repeatedly for cross-cutting strategies that involve development, law enforcement and interdiction, eradication, and the removal of implicated officials, but they have been just as frequently ignored—or at least, never implemented. These strategies would also require improved coordination among the government and the international communities' disparate civilian and military entities.

Rampant insecurity, corruption, and the increasing drug trade are strong indicators that Afghanistan has begun to slip back into a period of chaos and uncertainty. The Afghan people, whose hopes rose with the defeat of the Taliban and the prospect of a stable country, see their government as weak and corrupt. Never before has there been such hostility toward the United States within Afghanistan, and the goodwill brought by the United States [in 2001] has been all but squandered, said Landay. There is little time left to reach those people "still on the fence."

Good governance that actually delivers essential services is key to establishing a backbone of support within Afghanistan. Development aid must increase, and the Afghan government could benefit from an influx of development advisors to ensure that the available funds reach the crucial areas of the country. An increase in aid must be accompanied by measures to help ease the difficulty the Afghan government faces in actually spending the money. Bureaucratic bottlenecks and other delays that severely hamper the deliver of services by the ministries need to be resolved quickly to facilitate expanded funding by major donors to the government.

Expressing safety concerns for humanitarian workers, Alexander urged that indigenous community structures already in existence should be used to help foster sustainable development. The National Solidarity Program, widely viewed as a successful program to spur local development and governance, should be expanded and funded accordingly.

"The only solution is some kind of national unity." The two institutions that are symbolic of this concept are the Afghan National Army and the national parliament.

In order for the Afghan people to believe in their government, the international community must help re-establish the presence of the Kabul government throughout the country and especially in pro-Taliban areas. As a result of insufficient funds, many outlying provinces have yet to receive electricity and power. Government officials who attempt to establish their place in such provinces also lack basic necessities, such as building space and running water. An expanded road-building program, critical for both security and reconstruction, is extremely important to the Afghan people. "The legitimacy of the Afghan government is the ultimate and only solution," Thier asserted.

More International Forces

Participants underscored that the solution to the growing insurgency is not primarily a military one. Thinly deployed international troops do need reinforcements to stabilize the current climate of insecurity and to provide space for development and governance to grow. Lifting constraints imposed on troops through restrictive rules of engagement on the part of some participating NATO countries could help bolster security. The institutions that provide for rule of law—from the police to the judiciary—require serious attention. But according to Constable, many Afghans, whose tribal culture relies on deal-making to solve problems, believe that negotiation with the Taliban is the route to improved security. Any strategy to negotiate with the Taliban should be based on "the identification of true grievances amongst the people who must be won over," observed Thier. Other participants raised objections to negotiating with the Taliban and the Karzai government has yet to act on its stated policy to engage in serious dialogue.

The stability of Afghanistan is of utmost importance for the stability of the region. The recent peace deal between Pakistan and Waziristan has caused the Afghan public to question the credibility of Pakistan's partnership with the West to combat terrorism. The United States must put more concerted pressure on President [Pervez] Musharraf to take more active measures in dealing with insurgents. In addition, the United States should engage Iran by looking at regional stability in a more proactive way, said Alexander.

In a country that has been so "balkanized," observed Constable, "the only solution is some kind of national unity." The two institutions that are symbolic of this concept are the Afghan National Army and the national parliament, because their members do reflect the composition of Afghanistan's diverse society. This culture of institutions must spread throughout the country and provide governance, development, rule of law and security. The recent change in the Supreme Court and the Attorney General's office offer another sign of positive change. If the international community and the government of Afghanistan seize the opportunity now to build upon these successes, the window is still open—just barely—to ensure peace and prosperity.

NATO Must Commit to Afghanistan's Future

Bruce Riedel and Karl F. Inderfurth

Bruce Riedel is a senior fellow in foreign policy at the Saban Center for Middle East Policy. He has served as a senior advisor to three U.S. presidents on Middle East and South Asian issues. Karl F. Inderfurth is the John O. Rankin Professor of the Practice of International Affairs and the director of the Graduate Program in International Affairs at George Washington University in Washington, D.C. He also coauthored Fateful Decisions: Inside the National Security Council *and is a frequent op/ed contributor and commentator in the national media.*

More NATO (North Atlantic Treaty Organization) troops are needed in Afghanistan to ensure stability and continued development as well as safety from the Taliban. NATO must also fight the drug trade, which makes up almost fifty percent of the country's economy. Efforts to stabilize the borders and keep militants from entering Afghanistan must include cooperation with Iran and India, since no peace can be established without the help of sovereign countries in the region.

NATO defense ministers need to make some tough decisions about Afghanistan.... The violence in Afghanistan is four times more intense [in 2007] than it was [in 2006]. Suicide attacks have jumped from 27 in 2005 to 139 in 2006; the use of roadside bombs has doubled. Aid and reconstruction workers are targeted, setting back development efforts.

Bruce Riedel and Karl F. Inderfurth, "NATO Must Do More in Afghanistan," *Brookings Institution*, February 5, 2007. Reproduced by permission of The Brookings Institution.

First and foremost, more troops are needed.

The current level of 34,000 NATO soldiers in Afghanistan is only about 85 percent of what military commanders say they need. The outgoing NATO commander, General David Richards of Britain, has estimated that NATO is 4,000 to 5,000 troops short.

The United States, which contributes 12,000 troops to the NATO mission in Afghanistan and has another 12,000 personnel there under U.S. command, recently announced that it will keep 3,200 troops in Afghanistan for an extra four months to bolster NATO forces through the spring [of 2007]. Britain has said it will increase its overall deployment by 300.

These are positive responses, but they are not anywhere near enough....

More Troops

Secretary of Defense Robert Gates should announce that the United States is prepared to further increase the number of American troops in Afghanistan. That would reinforce the message Gates took ... to his first visit to NATO headquarters: "Success in Afghanistan is our top priority."

But success in Afghanistan must also become the top priority for NATO's other 25 members. The day after the Defense Department announced plans to extend the tour of U.S. soldiers in Afghanistan, Richards said he anticipated that at least another brigade of combat troops would be coming shortly from the other countries making up the international force in Afghanistan, and more after that. Yet the NATO secretary general, Jaap de Hoop Scheffer, seemed less certain, saying only that he is "relatively optimistic" that more troops will be forthcoming....

The United States and Britain should not bear the entire burden of increasing military forces in Afghanistan. NATO should also encourage its partners in the NATO Mediterranean dialogue, especially Egypt, Jordan, Tunisia, Algeria and Morocco, to offer troops to help stabilize Afghanistan.

Fighting the Drug Trade

Second, NATO must join in the fight against Afghanistan's exploding drug trade. Afghanistan is in danger of becoming a full fledged narco-state. The opium harvest rose by almost 60 percent in 2006, accounting for about 92 percent of the world's supply. Between a third and a half of Afghanistan's economy is dependent on the illegal drug trade. Drug proceeds are supporting the Taliban and helping fuel the growing insurgency.

To date, U.S.- and NATO-led forces have been reluctant to take part in combating the drug trafficking. But it is now clear that the Afghan Army, police and counternarcotics forces are not adequate to the job, and will not be for some time. NATO must assume a counter-drug mission.

> *NATO ... should ... set up a financial compensation program for civilian deaths, injuries or property damage resulting from NATO military operations in Afghanistan.*

Third, NATO should create a contact group led by a senior NATO diplomat to engage with all of Afghanistan's neighbors on ways to stabilize the borders, especially the 1,600 mile frontier with Pakistan. So long as the Taliban has a safe haven in Pakistan, it can continue [its] insurgency indefinitely.

NATO Must Win Over Afghanis

The contact group should include Iran, which has generally been help in Afghanistan (unlike in Iraq). NATO should also reach out to India, which has provided substantial aid for Afghanistan and has had a strong interest in being a partner in defeating Islamic extremism.

Finally, NATO's defense ministers should adopt the recent proposal by Human Rights Watch to set up a financial compensation program for civilian deaths, injuries or property damage resulting from NATO military operations in Afghanistan. [In 2006] at least 100 noncombatants were killed in air strikes or ground fighting.

On this, the hearts and minds of the Afghan people are at stake. Their continued support is critical for a foreign military presence in their country, a presence that may be needed for at least a decade to ensure that Afghanistan does not fall to extremist forces again.

NATO Must Help Afghanistan and Its Neighbors Cooperate

Joschka Fischer

Joschka Fischer, Germany's foreign minister and vice chancellor from 1998 to 2005, led Germany's Green Party for nearly twenty years.

The situation in Afghanistan is difficult and severe, but not yet hopeless. There is still time to help stabilize the central government. Yet Afghan forces need to be strengthened to fight the Taliban, and a more unified NATO (North Atlantic Treaty Organization) involvement is needed. Pakistan must also be a main focus, since the Taliban pose a threat to that country as well. NATO cannot give up on Afghanistan if it wants to stabilize the region and keep Europe and the world safe.

Things aren't going well in Afghanistan. Sometime at the turn of 2001/2002, the [George W.] Bush administration concluded that the stabilization and reconstruction of Afghanistan was no longer its top priority and decided to bet instead on military-led regime change in Iraq. Afghanistan can thus rightly be seen as the first victim of the administration's misguided strategy.

But the Bush administration is not the sole culprit for the deteriorating situation in Afghanistan. It was NATO's job to ensure the country's stability and security, and thus NATO's weak General Secretary and the European allies, especially Germany and France, share the responsibility for the worsening situation.

Joschka Fischer, "Afghanistan and the Future of Nato," *Project Syndicate*, 2007. Reproduced by permission.

There Is Still Hope

Yet, despite all the difficulties, the situation in Afghanistan, unlike that in Iraq, is not hopeless. There was a good reason for going to war in Afghanistan in the first place, because the attacks of September 11, 2001, originated there. Once undertaken, the West's intervention ended an almost uninterrupted civil war, and is still viewed with approval by a majority of the population. Finally, unlike in Iraq, the intervention did not fundamentally rupture the inner structure of the Afghan state or threaten its very cohesion.

If the West pursues realistic aims, and does so with perseverance, its main objective—a stable central government that can drive back the Taliban, hold the country together and, with the help of the international community, ensure the country's development—is still achievable.

There are four preconditions of the West's success:

- establishment of Afghan security forces strong enough to drive back the Taliban, limit drug cultivation, and create domestic stability;

- willingness on the part of NATO to remain militarily engaged without any national reservations—with Germany and France in particular giving up the special conditions of their involvement;

- a significant increase in development aid, especially for the so far neglected Southern part of the country;

- renewal of the regional consensus reached in Bonn [the Bonn Agreement] in 2001, under which the reconstruction of the Afghan state was to be supported by all the parties concerned.

Pakistan Shelters the Taliban

The war in Afghanistan was never just an Afghan civil war; rather, for decades the country has been a stage of regional conflicts and hegemonic struggles. So, while the rebirth of the Taliban is in part due to the woefully neglected reconstruction of the Pashto Southern and Eastern part of the country, it also has external causes. Most notably, for more than two years now, Pakistan has been moving away from the Bonn consensus, betting on the rebirth of the Taliban and giving it massive support. Indeed, without Taliban sanctuaries on the Pakistani side of the Afghan border, and without Pakistani financial backing, the rebirth of the Taliban's armed insurgency against the central Afghan government would have been impossible.

Pakistan's actions are explained mainly by its strategic readjustment in light of US weakness in Iraq and the region as a whole, and by the newly strengthened relationships between India and Afghanistan, resulting in an increased Indian presence in Central Asia. In this connection, Pakistan views the [Hamid] Karzai government in Kabul as unfriendly to [Pakistan's capital of] Islamabad and a threat to its key strategic interests. Without Taliban sanctuaries on the Pakistani side of the Afghan border and the backing by the Pakistani intelligence service ISI the rebirth of the Taliban's armed insurgency against the central Afghan government would have been impossible.

A regional consensus among all the players must be rebuilt, including Pakistan, Iran, and India, whose joint responsibility for peace, stability, and redevelopment in Afghanistan must be recognized by Europe and the US.

But, by aiding the Taliban, Pakistan is playing with fire, because there are now also Pakistani Talibans who pose a threat to Pakistan. US policy toward Pakistan is also dangerously shortsighted and reminiscent of the mistakes the US made in Iran prior to the 1979 Islamic revolution. Nevertheless, the US at least has a Pakistan policy—which is more than can be said about NATO and Europe. In fact, it is all but incomprehensible that while the future of NATO is being decided in the Hindu Kush mountains, and while thousands of European soldiers stationed there are risking their lives, Pakistan—the key to the success or failure of the mission in Afghanistan—is not given any role in NATO's plans and calculations.

NATO Has to Come Together

Part of NATO's trouble stems from the fact that a number of member states insist on the right to make their own military and political decisions, and these "national reservations" severely limit NATO's ability to act. If NATO is to succeed, this must change without further delay.

A NATO summit, during which all members would take stock of the situation and draw the appropriate conclusions, is therefore long overdue. The national reservations must go, and a joint strategy for success must be adopted, including a massive increase in civilian and military aid for Afghanistan, if the country is to be prevented from descending into the same abyss as Iraq.

Moreover, a regional consensus among all the players must be rebuilt, including Pakistan, Iran, and India, whose joint responsibility for peace, stability, and redevelopment in Afghanistan must be recognized by Europe and the US. To accomplish this, a follow-up conference to the Bonn Agreement is also required.

While the war in Iraq has been based on wishful thinking, the war in Afghanistan was necessary and unavoidable because it was there that the terrorist threat of September 11, 2001, originated. It would be more than a tragedy—it would be unparalleled political folly—if, because of a lack of commitment and political foresight, the West were to squander its successes in Afghanistan. Europe would have to pay an unacceptably high price, and NATO's future would likely be jeopardized.

The Course of U.S. Action Must Run Through Pakistan

Fred Kaplan

Fred Kaplan is Slate *magazine's War Stories columnist and the author of* Daydream Believers: How a Few Grand Ideas Wrecked American Power.

Taliban attacks have increased, and the situation in Afghanistan is deteriorating. At the core of the problem is America's lack of interest in the country. After the Soviets retreated in 1989, the United States left the country without help to establish a stable government, leaving the country to the Taliban. Even after the invasion in 2001 and the removal of the extremist regime, America squandered its early victories and is in danger of losing Afghanistan yet again to the Taliban. The only long-term solution is to bring the countries of the region together and negotiate an agreement among them. Unless this happens, the security of Afghanistan will be undermined by porous borders, conflicting interests in the region, and America's inability to safeguard the country.

What is going on in Afghanistan?

In [June 2008] Taliban fighters staged a prison raid and freed at least 1,000 of their brethren. Soon after, they mounted offensives on seven villages and are moving in on the southern stronghold of Kandahar. One of the fiercest Taliban lead-

Fred Kaplan, "The Taliban Are Back. What Now?" *Slate*, June 17, 2008. Distributed by United Feature Syndicate, Inc. Reproduced by permission.

ers, Maulavi Jalaluddin Haqqani, a major U.S. ally during the days of resistance to Soviet occupiers, is bringing in foreign jihadists from all over the region to help his cause.

Meanwhile, Taliban attacks are up considerably from [2007] despite increases in NATO [North Atlantic Treaty Organization] and Afghan troop levels. [General] Dan McNeill, who recently finished a 16-month tour as NATO commander in Afghanistan, said ... that we need 400,000 troops to control the country. There are now just 110,000 (including 58,000 from the still-green Afghan National Army) and few prospects for recruiting many more—*none* for remotely approaching McNeill's desired head count.

Finally, troop numbers mean little as long as Pakistan continues to give the Taliban fighters sanctuary in the Federally Administered Tribal Areas, just across Afghanistan's eastern border. And the [George W.] Bush administration has failed to convince the Pakistani authorities to crack down.

How did this disaster happen, and what is to be done about it now?

The disaster happened for a simple reason: The U.S. government—and this goes well beyond the Bush administration—has never given a whit about Afghanistan per se.

President Ronald Reagan and his CIA chief, William Casey, gave massive military assistance to the mujahedeen who were fighting off the Soviet occupiers. But once Mikhail Gorbachev withdrew his troops in 1989, Americans lost interest. The rest is dreadful history: The Taliban moved in, and so did Osama Bin Laden; the attacks of Sept. 11 followed.

Indifference Was a Mistake

In a sense, Reagan's indifference was understandable. The battle of the 1980s, as he (and, let's face it, nearly all of us) saw it, was a Cold War campaign. Afghanistan by itself was regarded as a backwater. The ultimate aims of our Islamist collaborators, and what they might do to the country afterward, were shrugged off.

The Course of U.S. Action Must Run Through Pakistan

One would think that subsequent presidents might have learned a lesson from the experience, but George W. Bush did not. CIA Director George Tenet and Defense Secretary Donald Rumsfeld mounted a brilliant campaign, along with Northern Alliance rebels, to oust the Taliban from Kabul and other Afghan cities. The regime fell in mid-November 2001, and Hamid Karzai's new government, backed by an international coalition, took office a month later. Remarkably, we once again moved on. *Some* U.S. troops stayed behind, but most of them—and nearly all intelligence assets—were transferred north to prepare for the invasion of Iraq.

The move was the product of an apolitical view of warfare—just as, 17 months later, President Bush would declare "mission accomplished" in Iraq on the grounds that Saddam Hussein had been ousted, ignoring the *strategic* goal of stabilizing a new, more democratic regime.

What is widely forgotten—and what was barely noticed by top U.S. officials at the time—is that the fiercest battle in that war, Operation Anaconda, occurred four months *after* the Taliban regime fell. And it was a very tough fight, in large part because Rumsfeld—believing the war was over—prohibited any units, even individual soldiers or Marines, from being sent to Afghanistan without his explicit permission.

Taliban Allowed to Regroup

Even after Anaconda, the Taliban didn't vanish; many of them merely retreated into the mountainous terrain along, or across, the Pakistani border. In the spring of 2006, NATO took over command, thinking it would be a "peacekeeping" operation—and, when the troops moved south, the Taliban came out and renewed the fight. (Several member-nations of NATO have declined to fight back because, when they signed on for the mission, they didn't think fighting was part of the deal.)

Pakistani border troops initially agreed to help out, battling the Taliban in the tribal areas. But the troops, who had never been trained for counterinsurgency combat, were outgunned and refused to fight on. The Pakistani military commanders, who saw Kashmir and India as bigger threats anyway, struck a separate deal by which they would go after al-Qaida jihadists in their midst but leave the Taliban alone.

This deal may not be even in their parochial interests, as the Taliban have been making gradual incursions ever deeper into Pakistan. However, Bush has squandered much of his leverage by siding with [Pakistan's] President Pervez Musharraf—and more intensely than ever, even as his standing in Pakistani politics has diminished. As Pakistan's ruling party, democratic movement, and even defense ministry have called on Musharraf to step down, [U.S.] Deputy Secretary of State John Negroponte has persisted in meeting with him and repeatedly expressing America's full support for him. Here was a rare occasion when U.S. moral values and material interests truly did coincide—and Bush, who has championed those values in his rhetoric, acted against both.

What to do now—or, more realistically, after January 20, 2009?

We ... have to help train and supply the Pakistani military to go after Taliban insurgents.

Above all, the new president will have to realize—as any military commander or regional specialist will tell him—that this is not a problem that can be solved within Afghanistan. We can keep fighting the Taliban—and probably keep them from retaking strategic positions—but it will remain at best a stalemate; we simply cannot amass enough troops to defeat them or stabilize the country.

A solution has to involve Pakistan. The Pakistani leaders, whoever they are, will not tackle the Taliban on the border unless they think that the mission is feasible and in their security interests. This is Political Science 101. So, we (or NATO or *some* group or groups of nations) have to help train and supply the Pakistani military to go after Taliban insurgents. We have to help relax tensions between Pakistan and India so that building up troops on the Afghan border won't seem to be a diversion. (Helping settle the two countries' dispute over Kashmir might be a start.) And we—in this case, the new American leaders—have to move away from Musharraf, whose future seems dim, and back the parliamentary leaders.

Finally, the security of Pakistan and Afghanistan—a subject that involves not just global terrorism, but nuclear weapons—is a regional issue. It was always a bit of a delusion, a post–Cold War dream, to think that NATO could handle this. The nations of the region have to be brought in—including Iran. The very phrase induces nightmares, but a "grand bargain" of some sort has to be struck. The nations involved in this bargain have so many disputes, so many conflicting interests, it is hard to imagine what the outlines of such a deal would look like. But it's very easy to imagine what kind of nightmare the alternative might look like. So there's no choice here; we have to try.

10

The United States Must Not Destabilize Pakistan

Jim Lobe

Jim Lobe is the Washington, D.C. bureau chief for Inter Press Service (IPS).

Events in Pakistan, such as the assassination of Benazir Bhutto and the rise of the Taliban, have led to increased U.S. military action in the country. Most Pakistanis who took part in a survey oppose these actions and many also felt the U.S. presence in the region was a threat to Pakistani interests. The new military intervention has led to fears of a destabilized country felt not only by Pakistanis, but by regional specialists as well.

Amid reports that the administration of U.S. President George W. Bush is considering aggressive covert actions against armed Islamist forces in western Pakistan, a new survey released Jan. 7 [2008] suggested that such an effort would be opposed by an overwhelming majority of Pakistanis themselves.

The survey, which was funded by the quasi-governmental U.S. Institute of Peace (USIP) and designed by the University of Maryland's Program on International Policy Attitudes (PIPA), also found that a strong majority of Pakistanis consider the U.S. military presence in Asia and neighboring Afghanistan a much more critical threat to their country than al-Qaeda or Pakistan's own Taliban movement in the tribal regions along the border with Afghanistan.

Jim Lobe, "Pakistanis See U.S. as Greatest Threat," *Washington Report on Middle East Affairs*, March 2008. Copyright © 2008 American Educational Trust. All rights reserved. Reproduced by permission.

The United States Must Not Destabilize Pakistan

Only 5 percent of respondents said the Pakistani government should permit U.S. or other foreign troops to enter Pakistan to pursue or capture al-Qaeda fighters, compared to a whopping 80 percent who said such actions should not be permitted, according to the poll, which was based on in-depth interviews of more than 900 Pakistanis in 19 cities in mid-September.

As a result, the survey did not take account of the tumultuous events that have taken place in Pakistan since then, including the six-week state of emergency declared by President Pervez Musharraf, the sacking of the Supreme Court, the return from exile of former Prime Ministers Benazir Bhutto and Nawaz Sharif, and Bhutto's Dec. 27 assassination which has led to the delay of scheduled parliamentary elections from Jan. 8 until February.

To what extent those events may have influenced public opinion in Pakistan on the range of issues covered by the survey—particularly toward the Pakistani Taliban, one of whose leaders, Baitullah Mehsud, has been accused by the government of carrying out Bhutto's killing—cannot be known.

Regional specialists both in and outside the administration have argued that such an intervention risked further destabilizing the country.

But the underlying attitudes revealed in the poll, especially toward the U.S., can offer very little comfort to the administration, which has become increasingly alarmed about recent events in Pakistan, particularly Bhutto's death, the Pakistani army's reluctance to take on the Taliban, and intelligence reports that al-Qaeda and its local allies, including the Taliban, have intensified their efforts to destabilize the government.

The Jan. 6 *New York Times* ran a front-page article regarding a White House meeting the previous Friday in which top officials, including Vice President Dick Cheney and Secretary of State Condoleezza Rice, reportedly debated pressing Musharraf and his new military leadership to permit the Central Intelligence Agency (CIA) and U.S. Special Operations Forces (SOF) to carry out more aggressive covert operations against selected targets in the Federally Administered Tribal Areas (FATA), the quasi-autonomous tribal areas that have come become increasingly dominated by the Pakistani Taliban, who have more recently extended their influence into the North West Frontier Province. The U.S. currently has about 50 soldiers in Pakistan acting primarily in an advisory and intelligence capacity.

While some administration officials reportedly believe that recent events have persuaded Musharraf and the army that they need such assistance to curb the growing Taliban–al-Qaeda threat, regional specialists both in and outside the administration have argued that such an intervention risked further destabilizing the country by triggering what the *Times* called "a tremendous backlash" against the U.S. and any government that was seen as its accomplice.

As to Pakistan-U.S. security cooperation, fewer than one in five respondents said it had either benefited Pakistan primarily or both equally.

Despite the nearly four-month hiatus since the USIP-PIPA survey was conducted, its findings would certainly appear to support the latter prediction.

While the survey found that a large majority of Pakistanis hold negative views of radical Islamists, including the Taliban and al-Qaeda, and strongly reject their use of violence against civilians, their views of the United States and its intentions toward Pakistan appear to be considerably more hostile and distrustful.

A whopping 84 percent said the U.S. military presence in the region was either a "critical" (72 percent) or an "important" (12 percent) threat to Pakistan's "vital interests."

By comparison, 53 percent of respondents said they believed tensions with India—with which Pakistan has fought several wars—constituted a "critical threat"; 41 percent named al-Qaeda as a "critical threat"; 34 percent put "activities of Islamist militants and local Taliban" in the same category.

Asked to choose from a list of alleged U.S. goals in the region, 78 percent cited Washington's alleged desire "to maintain control over the oil resources of the Middle East" (59 percent said it was "definitely" a goal, 19 percent said "probably"); 75 percent (53 percent "definitely") cited "to spread Christianity"; and 86 percent (70 percent "definitely") said it was "to weaken and divide the Islamic world." Only 63 percent (41 percent "definitely") chose the option "to prevent more attacks such as those on the World Trade Center in September 2001."

Moreover, a majority of respondents said they believed that the U.S. controls either "most" (32 percent) or "nearly all" (24 percent) of the recent major events that have taken place in Pakistan, compared to 22 percent who attributed "some" control to the U.S. and 4 percent who said "very little." Eighteen percent declined to respond.

As to Pakistan-U.S. security cooperation, fewer than one in five respondents said it had either benefited Pakistan primarily or both equally. Forty-four percent said it had mostly benefited the U.S.; and 11 percent said neither party had benefited.

Distrust of the U.S., however, did not translate into support for radical Islamists, the Taliban, or al-Qaeda, according to the survey. While they were considered much less of a threat than the U.S., 6 out of 10 respondents said they considered the Taliban and al-Qaeda either a "critical" or an "important threat" to Pakistan.

And even as huge majorities opposed any U.S. or foreign military intervention against the two groups in Pakistan, pluralities approaching 50 percent said they would support the Pakistani army entering the FATA to capture al-Qaeda fighters or Taliban insurgents who have crossed over from Afghanistan.

Comparable pluralities said they favored phasing out FATA's special legal status and integrating its areas into the country's overall legal structure, but also prefer taking a gradualist approach that includes negotiating with the local Taliban over using military force to impose the central government's control.

The survey also found overwhelming support for government based both on "Islamic principles" and on democratic ideals, including an independent judiciary and being governed by elected representatives. While 6 in 10 respondents said they supported a larger role for Islamic law, or *shariah*, in Pakistan's legal system, only 15 percent said they wanted to see more "Talibanization of daily life," a common phrase used in Pakistani media to refer to extreme religious conservatism.

Indeed, more than 8 in 10 said it was important for Pakistan to protect its religious minorities; more than three out of four said attacks on those minorities are "never justified"; and nearly two out of three said they support government plans to regulate religious schools, or *madrassas*, to require them to teach secular subjects, such as math and science. Only 17 percent said they oppose those reforms.

In general, those respondents who supported the expansion of *shariah* and government based on "Islamic principles" also tended to favor both democratic ideals and educational reforms at higher rates than others.

Covert Operations Cannot Substitute for Sound Policy

Patrick Cockburn

Patrick Cockburn is an Irish journalist who has been a Middle East correspondent since 1979 for The Financial Times *and, at present,* The Independent.

The covert U.S. military strikes along the Afghan border on Pakistani soil are part of the United States' problem in the region, not a solution. Air strikes have killed hundreds of civilians and create anger among the tribes of the region, while support for the Taliban increases. Without local support for the U.S. mission, however, any future covert action must fail. If the United States does not stop its current strategy, it will sacrifice long-term prospects for short-lived and disastrous military victories.

"Covert action is frequently a substitute for policy," was an aphorism first coined by the former director of the CIA Richard Helms. Its truth is exemplified by the decision of President [George W.] Bush in July [2008] to secretly give orders that US special forces will in future carry out raids against ground targets inside Pakistan, without getting the approval of the Pakistani government.

Mr Bush's order is fraught with peril for the US and NATO [North Atlantic Treaty Organization] forces in Afghanistan. In one respect, it is a recognition at long last by Mr Bush that the Taliban and their al-Qa'ida allies could not stay in busi-

Patrick Cockburn, "The US Strategy for Afghanistan Won't Work," *The Independent*, September 15, 2008. Reproduced by permission.

ness without the backing of Pakistan. This is hardly surprising, since it was Pakistani military intelligence which largely created them in the first place.

It was always absurd for the White House and the Pentagon to pour praise on the former Pakistani leader General Pervez Musharraf as their greater ally against terrorism, despite the clearest evidence that it was the Pakistani army which has been keeping the Taliban going since 2001.

Covert Action Kills Civilians

True to Helms's nostrum, Mr Bush has not adopted a new policy, but is resorting to covert operations, the political disadvantages of which are obvious, and military benefits dubious. A good example of this is the first of these operations undertaken under the new dispensation. On 3 September [2008], two dozen US Navy Seals were helicoptered in to South Waziristan in Pakistan, where they attacked a compound, aided by an AC-130 gunship. When they retreated, they said they had killed many al-Qa'ida fighters, though a senior Pakistani official later said that the true casualty figures were four Taliban and al-Qa'ida "foot soldiers" and 16 civilians, including women and children.

It is a curious way to usher in democracy in Pakistan.... It will create nothing but anger among Pakistanis. It will alienate the Pakistani army, which has been humiliated and disregarded. Politically, it only makes sense in terms of American politics, where it will be seen as a sign that the administration is doing something in Afghanistan. It also diverts attention from embarrassing questions about why the Taliban is such a potent force seven years after it had supposedly been destroyed in 2001.

Use of covert forces to achieve political ends with limited means has always held a fatal attraction for political leaders. CIA officials have become used to being dumped with insoluble problems, with peremptory orders to "Get rid of [former Iranian leader Ayatollah Ruhollah] Khomeini" or "Eliminate Saddam [Hussein]." Plots to do just that are the common theme of a thousand Hollywood movies, which revolve around the dispatch of elite forces into enemy territory, where they successfully dispatch some local demon.

In reality, covert warfare seldom works. Up-to-date intelligence is hard to come by. Take, for instance, the repeated claims by the US Air Force that it had killed Saddam Hussein during the US-led invasion of Iraq in 2003. This was meant to be based on up-to-the minute information, much of which turned out to be spurious. Of course Saddam had survived, though not the poor civilians who had the ill luck to live or work where the Iraqi leader was meant to be.

The Media's Nasty Role

The media plays a particularly nasty role in all of this. Stories of the attempts to kill Saddam Hussein were given maximum publicity. Their total failure was hardly mentioned. The reaction of the Pentagon to the killing of large numbers of civilians in Afghanistan, Iraq and now Pakistan has traditionally been first to deny that it ever happened. The denial is based on the old public relations principle that "first you say something is no news and didn't happen. When it is proved some time later, that it did happen, you yawn and say it is old news."

For some reason, the Israelis have a reputation for being good at undercover operations. This is hardly difficult in Gaza, where the enemy is so puny and vulnerable. But while I was stationed in Jerusalem for this newspaper, Israeli intelligence was involved in a series of ludicrous fiascos. My favourite was when the chief Mossad [Israeli intelligence] agent in Syria turned out not to exist, though his Israeli handler happily pocketed several million dollars that the spy was supposedly receiving for his treachery. The handler concocted the agent's reports and one of these, falsely claiming that Syria was plotting a surprise military offensive, even managed to get the Israeli army mobilised.

Covert operations only really succeed when they have strong local allies who want outside support.

Israel also provides a classic example of a covert operation that will produce limited gains if it is successful, and a diplomatic disaster if it is not. In September 1997, two Mossad agents carrying forged Canadian passports tried to assassinate Khaled Mashal, a Jordanian citizen, in the centre of the capital Amman. He was the head of the political bureau of [Islamist party] Hamas in Jordan. The ingenious method of assassination was to inject a slow-acting poison into his ear as he entered his office. In the event, the would-be poisoner was captured after a chase through the streets of Amman. Four other agents took refuge in the Israeli embassy.

The mission had been given the go-ahead by the Israeli prime minister of the day, Benjamin Netanyahu, who had simply ignored the idea that it might go wrong. King Hussein was reduced to threatening to storm the Israeli embassy unless Israel handed over an antidote to the poison. Israel was forced to release Sheikh Ahmad Yassin, the head of Hamas, and other Palestinian prisoners from jail.

Covert operations only really succeed when they have strong local allies who want outside support. There are two recent outstanding examples of this. In Afghanistan in 2001, US special forces reinforced the anti-Taliban Northern Alliance and, most importantly, gave them forward air controllers who could call in air strikes. Two years later, US special forces played a similar role in northern Iraq, when they provided air support to Kurdish troops attacking Saddam's retreating army.

But if covert forces are acting alone, they are very vulnerable. What will happen to them in Pakistan if they get in a fire fight with regular Pakistani forces? What will they do if they are ambushed by local tribesmen allied to the Taliban? Usually, the first to flee in these circumstances are the local civil authorities and the civilian population, so the Taliban will be even more in control than they were before.

Helms's dictum was right. The Bush administration got itself into a no-win situation in Afghanistan. "The US attack on Iraq," writes the Pakistani expert Ahmed Rashid, in his newly-published *Descent into Chaos*, "was critical to convincing Musharraf that the United States was not serious about stabilising the region, and that it was safer for Pakistan to preserve its own national interest by clandestinely giving the Taliban refuge."

The covert action in Pakistan is merely an attempt to divert attention from the consequences of this bankrupt American policy.

Organizations to Contact

The editors have compiled the following list of organizations concerned with the issues debated in this book. The descriptions are derived from materials provided by the organizations. All have publications or information available for interested readers. The list was compiled on the date of publication of the present volume; the information provided here may change. Be aware that many organizations take several weeks or longer to respond to inquiries, so allow as much time as possible.

The Brookings Institution
1775 Massachusetts Ave. NW, Washington, DC 20036
(202) 797-6000 • fax: (202) 797-6004
e-mail: brookinfo@brook.edu
Web site: www.brookings.org

The Brookings Institution is a think tank conducting research and education in foreign policy, economics, government, and the social sciences. Its publications include the quarterly *Brookings Review*, periodic *Policy Briefs*, and books, including *Terrorism and U.S. Foreign Policy*.

Center for Defense Information (CDI)
1779 Massachusetts Ave. NW, Suite 615
Washington, DC 20036
(202) 332-0600 • fax: (202) 462-4559
e-mail: info@cdi.org
Web site: www.cdi.org

CDI is a nonpartisan, nonprofit organization that researches all aspects of global security. It seeks to educate the public and policy makers about weapons systems, security policy, and defense budgeting. It publishes the monthly *Defense Monitor*.

Center for Strategic and International Studies (CSIS)
1800 K Street NW, Suite 400, Washington, DC   20006
(202) 887-0200 • fax: (202) 775-3199
Web site: www.csis.org

The center works to provide world leaders with strategic insights and policy options on current and emerging global issues. It publishes the *Washington Quarterly*, a journal on political, economic, and security issues, and other publications that can be downloaded from its Web site.

Central Intelligence Agency (CIA)
Office of Public Affairs, Washington, DC   20505
(703) 482-0623 • fax: (703) 482-1739
Web site: www.cia.gov

The Central Intelligence Agency was created in 1947 with the signing of the National Security Act by President Harry S. Truman. The CIA seeks to collect and evaluate intelligence related to national security and to provide appropriate dissemination of such intelligence. Publications such as its *Factbook on Intelligence* are available on its Web site.

Foreign Policy Association (FPA)
470 Park Ave. South, New York, NY   10016
(212) 481-8100 • fax: (212) 481-9275
e-mail: info@fpa.org
Web site: www.fpa.org

The FPA is a nonprofit organization seeking to inspire the American public to learn more about the world. The FPA serves as a catalyst for developing public awareness and understanding of, and providing informed opinions on, global issues. It publishes the *Great Decisions* DVD series and makes various articles and discussions available on its Web site.

The Heritage Foundation
214 Massachusetts Ave. NE, Washington, DC   20002-4999
(202) 546-4400 • fax: (202) 546-8328

e-mail: info@heritage.org
Web site: www.heritage.org

Founded in 1973, the Heritage Foundation is a research and educational institute whose mission is to formulate and promote conservative public policies based on the principles of free enterprise, limited government, individual freedom, and a strong national defense. It publishes many books on foreign policy, such as *Winning the Long War*.

Institute for Policy Studies (IPS)
733 Fifteenth Street NW, Suite 1020, Washington, DC 20005
(202) 234-9382 • fax: (202) 387-7915
Web site: www.ips-dc.org

The IPS is a progressive think tank working to develop societies built upon the values of justice and nonviolence. It publishes reports, including *Global Perspectives: A Media Guide to Foreign Policy Experts*. Articles are also available on its Web site.

National Security Agency (NSA)
9800 Savage Road, Ft. Meade, MD 20755-6248
(301) 688-6524
Web site: www.nsa.gov

The NSA coordinates, directs, and performs activities, such as designing cipher systems, which protects American information systems and produces foreign intelligence information. Speeches, briefings, and reports are available on its Web site.

Bibliography

Books

Ludwig Adamec — *Historical Dictionary of Afghan Wars, Revolutions, and Insurgencies.* 2nd ed. Lanham, MD: Scarecrow, 2005.

Tal Becker — *Terrorism and the State: Rethinking the Rules of State Responsibility.* Portland, OR: Hart, 2006.

Richard Clarke — *Defeating the Jihadists: A Blueprint for Action; The Report of a Task Force.* New York: Century Foundation Press, 2004

Steve Coll — *Ghost Wars: The Secret History of the CIA, Afghanistan, and Bin Laden, from the Soviet Invasion to September 10, 2001.* New York: Penguin, 2004.

Gilles Dorronsoro — *Revolution Unending: Afghanistan, 1979 to the Present.* New York: Columbia University Press in association with the Centre d'Etudes et de Recherches Internationales, Paris, 2005.

Martin Ewans — *Afghanistan: A Short History of Its People and Politics.* New York: HarperCollins, 2002.

——— *Conflict in Afghanistan: Studies in Asymmetric Warfare.* New York: Routledge, 2005.

Edward Girardet, Jonathan Walter, and Charles Norchi, eds.	*Essential Field Guides to Humanitarian and Conflict Zones: Afghanistan.* Rev. Ed. Geneva, Switzerland: Crosslines Global Report and Media Action International, 2003.
Larry Goodson	*Afghanistan's Endless War: State Failure, Regional Politics, and the Rise of the Taliban.* Seattle: University of Washington Press, 2001.
Salman Haidar, ed.	*The Afghan War and Its Geopolitical Implications for India.* New Delhi: Manohar, 2004.
Fred Halliday	*100 Myths About the Middle East.* Berkeley and Los Angeles: University of California Press, 2005.
Human Rights Watch	*All Our Hopes Are Crushed: Violence and Repression in Western Afghanistan.* New York: Human Rights Watch, 2002.
———	*Blood-Stained Hands: Past Atrocities in Kabul and Afghanistan's Legacy of Impunity.* New York: Human Rights Watch, 2005.
———	*"Killing You Is a Very Easy Thing for Us": Human Rights Abuses in Southeast Afghanistan.* New York: Human Rights Watch, 2003.

Bibliography

———	*"We Want to Live as Humans": Repression of Women and Girls in Western Afghanistan.* New York: Human Rights Watch, 2002.
Musa Khan Jalalzai	*Afghanistan, Central Asia, Pakistan and the United States.* Lahore, Pakistan: Bookbiz, 2003.
Ann Jones	*Kabul in Winter: Life Without Peace in Afghanistan.* New York: Metropolitan, 2006.
Ben Macintyre	*The Man Who Would Be King: The First American in Afghanistan.* New York: Farrar, Straus and Giroux, 2004.
Greg Mortenson and David Oliver Relin	Three Cups of Tea: One Man's Mission to Fight Terrorism and Build Nations . . . One School at a Time. New York: Viking, 2006.
Neamatollah Nojumi	*The Rise of the Taliban in Afghanistan: Mass Mobilization, Civil War, and the Future of the Region.* New York: Palgrave Macmillan, 2002.
Nelofer Pazira	*A Bed of Red Flowers: In Search of My Afghanistan.* New York: Free Press, 2005.
Ted Rall	*To Afghanistan and Back: A Graphic Travelogue.* New York: Nantier, Beall, Minoustchine, 2002.
Angelo Rasanayagam	*Afghanistan: A Modern History.* New York: I.B. Tauris, 2003.

Ahmed Rashid — *Taliban: Militant Islam, Oil and Fundamentalism in Central Asia.* New Haven, CT: Yale University Press, 2000.

Richard Rupp — *NATO After 9/11: An Alliance in Continuing Decline.* New York: Palgrave Macmillan, 2006.

Amin Saikal — *Modern Afghanistan: A History of Struggle and Survival.* New York: Palgrave Macmillan, 2004.

Periodicals

Jon Lee Anderson — "The Taliban's Opium War," *New Yorker*, July 9, 2007.

Associated Press — "Taliban Kills Two Sisters for Crime of Teaching," *New York Times*, December 10, 2006.

——— — "U.N.: Most Afghan Suicide Attacks Start in Pakistan," *Washington Post*, September 9, 2007.

Mike Blanchfield — "Timid Allies Endanger Canadian Troops, NATO Military Chief Henault Says," *Ottawa (ON) Citizen*, September 7, 2007.

Murray Brewster — "Top NATO Generals Meet in Canada to Map Afghanistan Strategy," *Canadian Press*, September 6, 2007.

Steven Cohen — "The Pakistan Time Bomb," *Washington Post*, July 3, 2007.

Anthony H. Cordesman	"Afghanistan on the Brink: Where Do We Go from Here?" Committee on Foreign Affairs, U.S. House of Representatives, 110th Cong., 1st Sess., February 15, 2007.
Andrew Feickert	"U.S. and Coalition Military Operations in Afghanistan: Issues for Congress," Congressional Research Service, March 27, 2007.
Roland Flamini	"Afghanistan on the Brink," *CQ Global Researcher*, June 2007.
Ejaz Haider	"Reconciling with Ground Realities," *Friday Times* (Lahore, Pakistan), August 17, 2007.
Ali A. Jalali	"The Future of Afghanistan," *Parameters*, Spring 2006.
Ali Jalali, Robert Oakley, and Zoe Hunter	"Combating Opium in Afghanistan," *Strategic Forum*, November 2006.
Seth Jones	"Averting Failure in Afghanistan," *Survival*, Spring 2006.
Ian MacDonald	"Picking a New Top Soldier," *Gazette* (Montreal), September 7, 2007.
Hayder Mili and Jacob Townsend	"Afghanistan's Drug Trade and How It Funds Taliban Operations," *Terrorism Monitor*, May 10, 2007.
Chandan Mitra	"J&K: Out of the Box," *Daily Pioneer* (New Delhi), September 13, 2007.

Ahmed Rashid	"Who's Winning the War on Terror?" *YaleGlobal*, September 5, 2003.
Susan Riley	"Downloading the War," *Ottawa (ON) Citizen*, September 5, 2007.
James Risen	"Poppy Fields Are New Front Line in Afghanistan War," *New York Times*, May 10, 2007.
David R. Sands	"Strikes on U.S., Afghan Forces Up Fourfold," *Washington Times*, January 17, 2007.
David Sanger and David Bohde	"U.S. Pays Pakistan to Fight Terror, but Patrols Ebb," *New York Times*, May 20, 2007.
UN Office on Drugs and Crime	"Afghanistan Opium Survey 2007: Executive Summary," August 2007.
Brian Glyn Williams	"The Taliban Fedayeen: The World's Worst Suicide Bombers?" *Terrorism Monitor*, July 19, 2007.
Robin Wright	"Iranian Arms Destined for Taliban Seized in Afghanistan, Officials Say," *Washington Post*, September 16, 2007.
Moeed Yusuf	"Tackling Pakistan's Extremists: Who Dictates, Us or Them?" Brookings Institution, September 6, 2007.

Index

A

Afghan National Army (ANA), 41, 64
Afghan National Liberation Front, 15–16
　See also Mojaddedi, Sibghatullah
Afghan National Police Program, 50–51
Afghanistan, 10, 24, 25
　civil war, 14, 60–62
　corruption/drug trade, 51
　counter-terrorism, 46
　democratically elected parliament, 47
　history of U.S. involvement, 30, 49–54, 59–60
　hostility towards westerners, 48
　infant mortality, 11
　international relief, 11–13
　nation building, 13–14, 19–20, 30, 49, 52
　resistance to centralized rule, 30–32
　system of laws, 14–15
　U.S. strategies, 18–22, 40–42, 45–49
　violence/killings against aid workers, 55
　See also Kabul; Karzai, Hamid; Mojaddedi, Sibghatullah
Afghanistan–Pakistan peace jirga, 36
Afghanistan Working Group, 49
Aizenstat, Jesse, 43–47
al Qaeda (terrorist network), 7–8, 37–40
al-Zawahiri, Ayman, 7, 40
Alexander, Deborah (U.S. embassy advisor), 49
Assassinations
　attempts against Karzai, 24
　of Benazir Bhutto, 68, 69
　against tribal leaders, 37

B

Bajpai, Kiya, 48
Bhutto, Benazir, 39, 68, 69
bin Laden, Osama, 7, 9, 64
bin Talal, Hussein (King of Jordan), 76
Blais, Jean-Jacques, 12
Bonn Agreement, 31, 41, 60–62
Brezhnev, Leonid (Soviet leader), 44
Burns, Nicolas, R. (U.S. Undersecretary of State), 33
Bush, George W.
　Afghanistan relations, 59, 65, 77
　Pakistan relations, 7, 64, 66, 68, 73–74
　tripartite meeting, 36

C

Casey, William (CIA chief), 64
Cheney, Dick (U.S. Vice President), 69
China, 21

87

CIA (Central Intelligence Agency), 27, 65, 70, 73, 74
Cockburn, Patrick, 73–77
Cole, Beth Ellen, 48–54
Constable, Pamela, 49, 51, 53
Covert operations
  consideration by Bush, 68, 73–74
  killing of civilians, 74–75
  role of media, 75–77
  U.S. Special Operations Forces, 70
Curtis, Lisa, 29–42

D

Democracy, 18, 50
  implications of, 12, 16
  in Pakistan, 74
  Taliban threats to, 23
  U.S. encouragement of, 43–47
Devendorf, George, 49, 50
Drought, 11–12

E

Education
  disruption of, 12
  restoration of, 16
European Union (EU), 20, 21

F

Federally Administered Tribal Areas (FATA), 34, 36–39, 70, 72
Fischer, Joschka, 59–62

G

Gates, Robert (U.S. Defense secretary), 46, 56
Germany, 26, 41, 46, 59–60
Gorbachev, Mikhail, 64

H

Haqqani, Maulavi Jalaluddin (Taliban leader), 64
Helms, Richard, 73, 74, 77
Human Rights Watch, 8, 57
Humanitarian workers, safety concerns, 52
Hussein, Saddam, 65, 75, 76

I

Inderfurth, Karl F., 55–58
India
  Afghanistan relations, 61–62
  bombing of embassy, 23–24
  border cooperation, 55
  NATO relations, 57
  Pakistan relations, 66–67, 71
  proposed summit including, 20–21
Insight on the News (magazine), 10, 12, 14, 15
International Committee of the Red Cross (ICRC), 24
International Security Assistance Force (ISAF), 40, 41, 51
Iran
  bilateral talks, 20
  border cooperation, 55
  influence on Afghanistan, 33–34
  NATO relations, 57, 67
  U.S. strategy, 28, 53, 61–62
Iraq
  bombing tactics, 26, 33, 48
  covert operations, 76
  insurgency, 34
  Iran relations, 33
  media's role, 75
  NATO relations, 57, 62
  Pakistan relations, 61

U.S. intelligence on, 75
U.S. strategy, 9, 28, 45, 59–60, 65, 77
U.S. withdrawal, 17, 20, 22
Israel, 75–76

J

Jalali, Ali (Minister of Interior), 13

K

Kabul, 12, 23, 31, 33, 46
    Afghanistan-Pakistan peace jirga, 36
    government reestablishment, 52–53
    Soviet defeat of, 44–45
    Taliban's expulsion from, 45, 65
    U.S. rebuilding support, 49
    See also Karzai, Hamid
Kaplan, Fred, 63–67
Karzai, Hamid (President of Afghanistan), 12–15, 19, 24, 31, 48, 50, 53, 61
Khomeini, Ayatollah Ruhollah, 75

L

Land mines, 11–12, 34
Landay, Jonathan (journalist), 49, 50, 52
Lobe, Jim, 68

M

Mahmood, Muhammad Malam, 15
Mashal, Khaled (Chief of Hamas), 76

Mayor of Kabul. *See* Karzai, Hamid
McCain, John, 43
McKiernan, David (NATO Commander), 27
McNeill, Dan (U.S. General), 64
Media, role of, 75–76
Meshrano Jirga, 32
Missile attacks, 7–9, 25
Mojaddedi, Sibghatullah, 15–16
Mr. Commission. *See* Karzai, Hamid
Musharraf, Pervez (Pakistan President)
    actions against insurgents, 53, 69–70
    peace deal with tribal leaders, 37
    support of Afghan militants, 36
    U.S. relations, 21, 66–67, 74, 77

N

National Solidarity Program, 52
NATO (North Atlantic Treaty Organization)
    Afghanistan relations, 51, 53, 55–56, 60
    Afghanistan strategy, 18, 20–21, 59, 64–65, 73
    border control, 26–27
    insurgent tactics, 50
    limited ability to act, 62
    loss of support, 26
    Mediterranean relations, 56–57
    Pakistan relations, 61–62, 66–67
    soldier costs, 42

Netanyahu, Benjamin (Isreali Prime Minister), 76
Netherlands, 46
New York Times (newspaper), 8, 69
9/11. *See* September 11, 2001 attack
Nongovernmental organizations (NGOs), 12–13, 50
Noorzai, Mohamed Arif (Frontier Tribal Affairs Minister), 13, 14
North Waziristan, 7, 8, 26, 37, 53
Northern Alliance (anti-Taliban warlords), 45, 65, 76

O

Obama, Barack, 43
Operation Anaconda, 65
Operation Enduring Freedom (OEF), 40

P

Pakistan, 7, 25, 26, 65–72
    Afghanistan-Pakistan peace jirga, 36
    Bush administration relations, 7, 68, 73–74
    cooperation with the U.S., 38–39
    helicopter attack by U.S., 8
    involvement of foreign insurgents, 27–28, 34
Pew Global Attitudes Project, 26
Phillips, James, 29–42
Politburo (Soviet ruling body), 44
"The Professor." *See* Mojaddedi, Sibghatullah
Program on International Policy Attitudes (PIPA), 68, 70

R

Rashid, Ahmed, 77
Reagan, Ronald (U.S. President), 64
Red Army (Soviet Union), 44
Rice, Condoleezza (U.S. Secretary of State), 70
Richards, David (U.S. General), 56
Riedel, Bruce, 55–58
Rodriquez, Paul M., 10–16
Rogers, Paul, 23–28
Rubin, Elizabeth, 8
Rumsfeld, Donald (U.S. Defense Secretary), 65
Russia. *See* Soviet Union

S

Sadqee, Mohammed, 15
Scheffer, Jaap de Hoop, 56
Schloesser, Jeffrey J. (Major-General), 26
September 11, 2001 attack, 9, 42, 60, 62, 64
Sharif, Nawaz, 69
South Waziristan, 26, 34, 74
Soviet Union
    Afghanistan defeat of, 15–16, 63–64
    defeat of Herat and Kabul, 44–45
    invasion by Taliban, 9
    Politburo, 44
    See also Brezhnev, Leonid
Special Operations Forces (SOF), 70
Syria, 75

T

Taliban (terrorist network), 8–9, 19, 23, 25–28, 65, 73–74
Tenet, George (CIA Director), 65
Thomson, Denis (brigadier-general), 44
Thurston, Alex, 17–22
Tribal issues
    al Qaeda sanctuary, 38
    assassination of local leaders, 37
    culture, 14, 31, 45, 53
    deployment of military, 37
    NATO relations, 61–62
    Pashtun tribal areas, 30, 38
    peace deal with leaders, 37
    strategy, 32–33, 45
    survival based traditions, 14
    Taliban relations, 64
    terrorist training camps, 37
    U.S. invasion, 39
    U.S. repeal of aid, 48
    See also Federally Administered Tribal Areas; Musharraf, Pervez

U

United States (U.S.), 7–9, 12
    Afghanistan strategy, 18–22, 34–35, 40–42, 45–49
    cooperation with Pakistan, 38–39, 63
    democracy encouraged in Afghanistan, 43–47
    historical involvement in Afghanistan, 30, 49–54, 59–60
    intelligence on Iraq, 75
    invasion of Pakistani tribal area, 39
    Iran strategy, 28
    Iraq strategy, 9, 28, 45, 59–60, 65, 77
    Musharraf relations, 21, 67, 74, 77
    rebuilding efforts in Afghanistan, 13–14, 19–20, 30, 49, 52
    U.S. led coalition failure, 29–30
    withdrawal from Iraq, 17, 20, 22
U.S. Agency for International Development (USAID), 50
U.S. Department of State, 50
U.S. Institute of Peace (USIP), 49

W

Warlords, 12, 15, 31, 45, 51
Wolesi Jirga, 32

Z

Zaman, Shah (citizen), 7

www.ingramcontent.com/pod-product-compliance
Lightning Source LLC
Chambersburg PA
CBHW072103290426
44110CB00014B/1798